Inspiring Independence

Inspiring Independence

Seven Steps for Helping Executive
Directors Achieve Independence
for Their Clients

SUSAN BEAIRD

Inspiring Independence, LLC
Germantown, Tennessee

Inspiring Independence, LLC
Germantown, Tennessee
Copyright © 2025 by Susan Beaird. All rights reserved.
Library of Congress Control Number: 2025924302
Paperback ISBN: 979-8-9937143-0-1
Ebook ISBN: 979-8-9937143-1-8

Book cover and interior design by Christina Thiele
Editorial production by KN Literary Arts

To Letty—mentor extraordinaire

*To Dina—for your weekly encouragement and belief in
my ability to actually pull this off*

*To my Sis—for always being my champion and coming up
with loving advice in all the right moments*

To Michelle—without whom this book might never have been

Contents

Introduction

$\mathcal{M}$y journey from powerless female to independent woman was long, rocky, and muddy. Despite the detours and wrong turns, I pressed on to learn the experience of self-love and the power of passion and courage in my beliefs. I started my adult life thinking I had to replicate my father's business career but later realized my mother's volunteer work in the nonprofit world was much closer to my own passion. Then, after a divorce, I began the decades-long therapeutic journey that brought me to today and enabled me to complete the consummation of my work life—this very book. It was through this journey that I learned and accepted that I'm, in fact, a Wonder Woman! But in deference to DC Comics, I will use the moniker *Independent Woman*.

Helping women find their independence is my passion. Specifically I love working with those who have struggled as I have with a lack of confidence in their overall abilities and survival skills. Because of this, I hope to use the following pages to support and guide you in your role as executive director of a social service nonprofit. I want to show you how your status as a successful and independent woman can be passed on to your clients.

While I could have directed this book into the ether to women globally, I picked you—the woman running a small, socially missioned nonprofit directly serving women—because my experience aligns with yours. There are a gazillion books that can help you build your organization so that it survives and thrives. There are just as many self-help books, a slew of which I've read over the years, that can greatly augment your journey toward a healthy life. *Inspiring Independence* stands apart from the crowd firstly due to my nearly four decades of experience and secondly in how it bridges the gap between self-help insights and their real-world application to your job as an executive director. The advice in these pages is about character building, facing the inner struggles that come with the job, and engaging with the inner struggles of the women coming through your door. Throughout the seven steps detailed in this book, I'll be your *supporter, friend, coach,* and *mentor*—the same roles you fill daily with your colleagues and the women who come to your organization. Each of these roles has a different purpose, but amazingly, they are all a necessary part of your job as an executive director.

I chose to title this book *Inspiring Independence* because I wanted it to capture the fortitude, resilience, and confidence of a woman who's dedicated her life to helping other women find their freedom and thrive. That woman is you—the executive director of a nonprofit. In my eyes, that makes you nothing short of a Wonder Woman. If you're familiar with the DC tale, then you know Wonder Woman was as beautiful as Aphrodite, as wise as Athena, stronger than Hercules, and swifter than Mercury. She left her Greek island paradise to fight fascism from America, the last citadel of democracy and equal rights for women. I may not be the fabled character you see in the movies, nor a political trailblazer like Hillary Clinton, or a cultural icon like Oprah—the world already holds one of each, each unique in their own right. But just as there's only one of them, there's only one of you and one of me.

The time I've devoted to the social services missions of the nonprofit world has shown me that seeing the women who lead them and the clients they serve *transformed into independent women is my passion.* What moves me to my core is the independence of all women. My hope is to see you and your clients thrive, bright with energy, secure in a job you love and financially rewarded for it. *Inspiring Independence* is my attempt to draw you a picture of life as an independent woman with her red-and-black outfit and superhero powers that allow her to leap over tall buildings and defeat her enemies. These enemies can be *inside* ourselves or *outside.* In truth, this book is mainly about the inner work it takes to climb the ladder from helpless and hopeless to independent woman, for this was my journey.

I've not only been an executive director, I've also had the privilege to know and work with many nonprofit directors over the last 40 years. As an executive director, you're part of a special breed of women who carry your gift of nurturing into the workplace and serve it up to your staff and clients daily. Your job is so complex it's like a kaleidoscope of distinct colors that rely on each other. You're the inspirer, the encourager, the planner, the leader and the overseer—all in one. Your job constantly changes and morphs into new challenges and daily puzzles like how to make that income figure balance with the expenditures and the "simple" task of fitting in family, work time, and me-time into each 24 hours. Sitting at the plain wooden school desk donated by an elementary school that closed nearby, you draw up your list of must-dos for the day. Very little deliberation is possible because your door opens and a volunteer wants to know what she should focus on today. Meanwhile, the phone rings: someone returning the call you made yesterday to see if a similar program down the road would consider sharing your space to save you both money. And so it goes day after day until it's time to stop everything and meet with the nonprofit's board of directors for help raising much-needed funding to keep the organization afloat for another six months.

As an executive director, you take this demanding, exhausting job because of a passion to serve that can't be denied. Perhaps you even got into this job as a client first. If so, you uniquely understand the worth of the nonprofit's effort because it brought you out of your helplessness and hopelessness into a life of productive giving to others. Or, perhaps, you got into what you thought was just a job only to have it grab your heart and refuse to let go. Either way, it's no longer just a job—it's a fulfillment of a longing you, like me, may not even have realized you had.

Not only does *Inspiring Independence* take from my personal experience of forming, running, and consulting for nonprofits, it also reflects my experience coaching executives, as well as the experience of executive directors past and present who graciously allowed me to share their wisdom throughout the book. In the following pages, you'll come to learn what I call the **Seven Steps to Independence.** These steps are aptly named, for when mastered, you'll know your true worth and power:

- Step 1: **Acknowledging Your Limits**
- Step 2: **Seeing Your Choices**
- Step 3: **Owning Your Abilities**
- Step 4: **Letting Your Passions Guide You**
- Step 5: **Building on Your Success**
- Step 6: **Recognizing Your Independent Woman Status**
- Step 7: **Passing It On**

I hope you read this until the pages are yellow with age and the underlines are like stripes on a bass. I want it to feed you spiritually, mentally, and emotionally so you can go out into the world ready to face the rocky road ahead and embrace what it has to offer you and the women you serve.

Are you ready to set off on your unique journey? Perhaps that means slowly putting one foot in front of the other, pedaling on a trusty bicycle with an occasional push from others, or even bumping along in your old, broken-down jalopy that may or may not start. However you go forward, keep pushing on because your heart, not just your head, must see what's at the end of that rainbow. You can't give up because you know deep down that, to fulfill your mission, you'll have to navigate whatever turns or steep banks lie ahead.

If others have done it, you, too, can do it in your own unique way. You can be a true independent woman!

STEP ONE

Acknowledging Your Limits

$\mathcal{M}$y path to becoming an independent woman began with years of pain and frustration in my early adult life. I felt trapped, unseen and unattended to, but even that part of my journey was part of the learning process. You can't become an independent woman without understanding helplessness. For me to gain traction and move on, my belief system had to break out of that sense of hopelessness, that feeling of being a captive of my circumstances. Like the little engine that could, I had to believe going forward was possible before I'd have the courage to try. But, I was imprisoned in my own bed of helplessness, feeling out of control and unable to do anything about my situation. Gradually, though, I began to believe in my voice, experience, and wisdom from the journey and accept who I'd been all along—an independent woman. Had I never experienced the breakout, I would have remained stuck, limited by nothing more than that voice in my head. A different perception of myself was essential to transition to Wonder Woman—an exciting, vivacious, momentous, confident woman with the ability to change the world.

Having my eyes opened to see what was there all along has taken at least 50 years, but it's been worth it because my journey can now impact others. The same can be true for you. No, your transformation may not be a steady climb. You may even find rungs missing from your ladder from time to time. Still, hopefully, by surrounding yourself with positive people and trying things you thought were impossible, you'll reinforce your ability to see the change that's possible.

If you're feeling stuck, ask yourself, "If things were completely different, what would I do with my life? What would I try to adjust to bring about change in my life?" Sometimes, it takes only one voice or action, like climbing a formidable mountain, to admit to ourselves that we're not a complete failure and have the skills we need to open doors to reveal our hidden passions.

Belief in ourselves is how you and I get the courage to trudge on in the dark, to right ourselves and keep going after we stumble, even though we certainly can't see the next turn or resting place. We must believe that if we keep looking, the path will somehow show itself. We must trust that if we keep searching and refuse to give up despite our uncertainty, all things are possible. To reach the top of the mountain, we must push on, taking our tiny steps so we can help others who are on their way up. That's what it takes to reach the summit.

Sit Still and Look Pretty

I was born into privilege. My mother was a full-time volunteer and housewife and my father was the head of the household and the breadwinner. His wishes were paramount because he ultimately brought home the bacon. She deferred to him in things as small as his meal or movie choices to more significant things like vacations or housing. Being the firstborn and a girl,

I was expected to be mostly silent and do as I was told, make straight As in school, behave, and always look pretty. There was never any discussion about what choices I might make in life. Suffice it to say, not many careers outside of teaching, nursing, secretarial work, or being a housewife were available to women in the '40s and '50s. So, there was no talk at our dinner table about what I wanted to be when I grew up. But in the case of my younger brother, the third child and "prince charming," the sky was the limit! In Brené Brown's book *I Thought It Was Just Me* she writes, "In current research, women are judged as to appearance and motherhood, whereas men are sized up by monetary success, intellect and physical strength, all measures of power."[1] These discrepancies are thankfully not as prominent today. There are certainly more women in leadership positions than in those days when the prince charmings were the only ones in the family who were thought capable of meaningful employment.

Since our back gate opened onto my elementary school's property, I walked to class. My least favorite class was gym, so I particularly disliked Field Day. Southfield School was known for special event days like Kite Day, Field Day, and May Day. Field Day was when the whole school was brought outside onto the large grass-covered area behind the school for a series of track and field events. There were relay races, races over hurdles, sack races, etc. Some of my classmates may have loved the event, but to me, Field Day was simply a reminder that because I was a girl and small for my age, I was going to be picked last for any athletic activity. For some reason, they determined that my short legs could make it over the hurdles.

Now, really! Were they set on seeing me fail? The entire event was mortification personified.

In college, I was elected a "beauty," further enforcing my image as a pretty but useless girl. Combined with my childhood experiences, this served to place my poor self-esteem at the forefront of my impression of myself. In therapeutic language, what I was subject to is termed abuse, even if it was mental and not physical. The resulting damage was just as harmful and led to the same lack of self-worth and negative and hopeless thoughts that physical abuse would have inflicted. However, as the years passed and I found my place in the nonprofit arena, I began to imagine that as a woman with brains and looks, maybe I could become valuable to society if not yet an independent woman. For me, this mental transformation mirrors a butterfly's metamorphosis—from an egg to a caterpillar, then from a chrysalis to a vibrant creature who can finally spread its wings.

Like a caterpillar, we must first crawl around and consume all the information the world offers. Then, we form into a chrysalis and internally ruminate on what is us and what isn't. Once we emerge as a butterfly with strength and power, we can fly wherever our passions guide us. As a caterpillar, I subjected myself to all the abuse I was hearing that told me "You aren't worthwhile, smart, athletic, accomplished, famous, or contributing to a better world." But eventually, through trial and error, success and failure, I learned what I needed to turn into that butterfly with a cape for wings, soaring as an independent woman.

The caterpillar stage.

The Heart of Poverty

Would you believe me if I told you that there are attributes of poverty that have nothing to do with money? When asked how he defined poverty, Peter K. Greer, CEO of HOPE International, said, "Poverty is an empty heart, not knowing your abilities and strengths, not being able to make progress, isolation, no hope or belief in yourself, knowing you can't take care of your family ... (and) lack of good thoughts."[2] Deepa Narayan with the International Monetary Fund, an organization that's done extensive worldwide research on poverty reduction and economic management, added to Greer's insights in an article titled "Poverty is Powerlessness and Voicelessness." In the article, Narayan wrote, "Poor people need assets to reduce their vulnerability ... (They) know that their survival depends on resources controlled by others." [3]

She went on to outline needs like healthcare, explaining that poor people's organizational abilities for such needs rarely extend further than their family and community. Additionally, information about their rights as workers and about jobs or assistance programs, education, and protection for ideas and entrepreneurship was sorely lacking.

These youngsters in Masvingo, Zimbabwe, are lining up to get a free porridge that is rich with the nutrients they need.

My trip to Zimbabwe, Kenya, Tanzania, and Rwanda in 2017 reinforced my observations and experience with the women who come to social service nonprofits for guidance, strength, and training. Although I don't believe in putting folks in boxes, the traits Greer and Narayan detailed are far too common in women who find themselves powerless and struggling to find their voice and gain security—all they see is their limits rather than what IS possible. Amazingly, you, as executive director, can have that same limited belief structure.

In Erik Hanberg's *The Little Book of Nonprofit Leadership*, he states that an executive director's job can be divided into three areas: the mission, the people, and the money. He writes that executive directors are there either for the "love of the money, paltry as it usually is, love of the mission, or to serve the community." Because an executive director's job is leadership first and foremost, some might ask, "Who do they lead?" Well, the community, the staff, and the volunteers, of course. But, most importantly and trickily, you also lead the board that hired you. As Hanberg humorously observed, your job is essentially "like herding cats."[4]

I've heard from many executive directors over the years who wrestled with limiting beliefs about their skills and abilities, thanks to everything their job requires them to juggle. Some were convinced that whoever formed their program was just smarter or more capable. Others believed that they didn't have all the skills or credentials they needed to do a good job for their clients, even though it was clear to me that they were doing an excellent job.

The "missing skills" on my site visits sounded something like this:

- I don't have the background in counseling that I need to help these women.
  - **The good news:** Counseling skills can be pulled from your personal experience, even without formal training. Advise your clients as if you would advise a close friend. You have more wisdom than you know!
- I don't know how to run a business like a nonprofit.
  - **The good news:** As the executive director, you can rely on expertise from more experienced colleagues in your area and training courses from organizations like LANO (Louisiana Association for Nonprofits) for the fiscal details you need to run the show.
- I have so many bosses.
  - **The good news:** You have your board, the community, and even your staff and clients to report to, but you'll learn how to manage and somehow thrive despite it.
- I'm not sure how to be a good leader.
  - **The good news:** You don't have to stay in your office all day. Make sure your staff sees you daily and that you make yourself available to them, your board and, ultimately, the community.
- I don't know how to prevent the burnout that others I know have dealt with.

- **The good news:** Prioritizing breaks changes everything. Even 10 minutes in the park can help clear your head. Setting aside wellness days for you and your staff will show that everyone needs rest from the grind.

In *The Executive Director's Guide to Thriving as a Nonprofit Leader*, Mim Carlson and Margaret Donohoe deem you, the executive director, as the supreme caretaker of your organization. As Carlson and Donohoe write in their book, "When you are a leader, you work from the heart ... as a manager, you work from the head."[5] Executive directors are managers and leaders who serve multiple entities: the board, the community, and the participants needing their guidance. To do this effectively, you must be "a visionary, a change agent, a relationship builder, a community creator and a resource wizard."[6] Sounds easy-peasy, right? With so many roles, you really are expected to be an independent woman. But even you come face to face with limits at times, don't you? You may be an independent woman, but you're still human. That said, your greatest limits will always be those you place on yourself—the ones you perceive. It's easy to get stuck believing what others say about your skills. It's just as easy getting trapped in the old lies you've told yourself. I know you may not feel like it some days, but you are both a leader and a manager and I'm going to prove it to you in the following chapters.

To help you discover the limits you've placed on yourself, let's play a fun mental game like the one I used to play as a child after supper in the summer—Hide and Seek. I remember hiding in such places as behind rocks, behind trees, in a cabinet, or under the bed. Let's pretend that each hiding place represents a fear or lie that you believe about yourself. For me, rocks might represent hard stuff to admit—mistakes and failures, and trees would be me unwilling to be as vulnerable as necessary to tell this story completely. Now, a kitchen cabinet would be a box of self-hate, self-denial of my gifts, talents, and skills that I don't necessarily value but others see as exciting, useful, and creative. Being under the bed would be me trying to be as small as possible instead of putting out my chest with "independent woman" written in bold red and black. Now we always hear when the "It" person gives up, someone cries, "Ollie ollie oxen free!" This cry, of course, signals that it's time to come out of hiding. As in the game, you and I must step out of hiding and embrace our true selves. Who is the REAL YOU? My rocks were the multiple businesses I started. My trees took me from a for-profit company to the world of non-profit organizations, where I now thrive. My cabinets and beds gave me the self-assurance to move on to coaching, consulting, and writing this book.

Now it's your turn. What are your rocks, trees, cabinet, and bed? And what have they led you to now? Make a list of the things that limit you. What factors are preventing you from being your best self or giving all you can? Begin to imagine how you might eliminate some of these obstacles.

A Glimmer of Hope

As you've probably already experienced, your clients struggle with feeling limited and helpless even more than you do. These women are often low-income, sometimes homeless, living in cars or on the street, abandoned and financially insecure. They've been told what second-class citizens they are from so many directions that they typically don't have any role models who escaped similar situations. They've lived in their neighborhood their whole lives, barely able to put food on the table, with no stability or education to qualify for a job that pays decently. Many times, they can feel stuck physically and emotionally, brainwashed into thinking that they don't have options. They ask questions like, "How would I get to a program or work? I can't even afford a car." In *Living the Abundant Life: 9 Principles to Move from Poverty to Prosperity*, author Sylvia O'Connor calls this attitude short-term thinking because it focuses on tangible scarcity rather than the abundant possibilities that could be. As she notes, "Getting rid of a poverty mindset is an ongoing process."[7]

So, if both you and your clients struggle with a poverty mindset, how do you move toward believing what could be? Believe it or not, Brené Brown writes in *The Gifts of Imperfection* that this poverty mindset can be changed with a short but powerful word—*hope*. Hope can be learned by knowing where we want to go and believing we can get there. Many a strong, independent woman has told me about her working mother teaching her that she could do anything she set her mind upon. If only we all could have had that belief system in our households. But sadly, it's relatively rare. Thankfully, it can be learned and recognized in ourselves. When it comes to helping your clients, the first thing you can do as the executive director is to point out all your participants' options. Paint them a picture of hope with realistic endings and outcomes. Help them pinpoint their limiting beliefs and imagine their future accomplishments. And, most importantly, *have fun*!

The Secret To Getting Back Up

In the early '70s, I was struggling to get a paralegal job. Becoming a paralegal was not what I went to school for, but I'd scored so low on the law entrance exam that even with Daddy's pull in Shreveport, I couldn't get into law school. So, I decided to see if I even liked the law by working as a paralegal. While searching for a job, I interviewed with the hiring group of every law firm in Shreveport. Dressed in my best business attire, I answered dumb questions like, "What in the heck is a paralegal?" In those days, only two schools in the country offered majors in this discipline, so many of these attorneys had no idea what the position they were interviewing for entailed. They were sure I was trying to take one of their jobs and my being a woman made hiring me even more difficult for them to swallow. Since they all knew my daddy, I often got a polite "Thank you, but no thank you," leaving me feeling ostracized and rejected because I didn't fit into the old boys' club. This venture is just one early example of my "failures" that led me to another learning experience.

When I saw how limited I was by my gender and how the

old boys' club was fueling the insecurity I abhorred, I vowed to find a way around this societal view by getting into a world that mostly valued women the same as men—the nonprofit arena. As I grew to know and love the nonprofit world, I realized that my feelings of failure and non-belonging were nowhere near as extreme as those of most social services clients I served. The exclusion from society through poverty and isolation had created a much worse belief of "I am lacking" than had my not fitting into the old boys' club. Still, my experience came with a similar loneliness and sense of vulnerability. In a way, I understand how they felt. In trying to fit into the paralegal world, my heart had been saying the same thing as theirs—"I clearly don't belong!"

In *Rising Strong*, Brené Brown explains that owning "our stories of falling down, screwing up and facing hurt" is necessary to "integrate those stories into our lives and write a daring new ending."[8] This vulnerability surrounding our failures isn't only worth it but essential to success. Of course, we'll feel weak, like the sky will fall in, or that no one will ever give us a shot. But we must be willing to fail! Even with all the negative voices in our heads, the naysaying neighbors, and the grim statistics we're up against, a new ending to our story is always possible.

The real secret to my trying over and over again is *my passion*. When that passion aligns with who you are, it's unstoppable, impregnable, and so bold that you must try. To keep going, we must give it our best shot because we care too much about why we are doing this thing. We must give it a go and see if we can make it come to life, make it out there, make it tangible, make it real, and make it authentic. The mission is core to who we are, coming from a place deep inside that *must* manifest itself. It must see the light of day no matter what anyone else says or thinks.

There is a passion within each of us that drives us, inspires us and causes us not to weigh possible failures but to press on ahead into the unknown with that light of passion leading our way. When we find the work our soul craves, the old saying, "If you love your work, it's not work," rings true and we will want to pass on our understanding of how to find that passion.

The Client Path

It's not hard for me to know I landed on the right path. Looking back, it's easy to see I didn't fit in the legal world. I would have hated law and never truly shone in that field because I didn't see the little things, just the big picture, and that wasn't the job. Imagine how much more intense the "I don't fit" feeling is for your clients. The rest of the world is out there, but when they're not allowed entrance, struggling financially and poorly educated, everything feels like it's for everyone *but* them. Add in not having a roof over their head, and these clients on the streets or living out of their cars feel like life has started them off with a double whammy. Their fight is even more challenging in some ways because they are truly at the bottom. But here is where their upward journey can begin. After all, they don't have any way but up.

By bravely and vulnerably acknowledging your limitations and how you overcame them, you enable them to get a glimpse of their possible path out of their current condition into one of security and safety. As it is for most of us, security is paramount to your clients. In their minds, security is the same as survival. Feeling unsure of their survival will keep them blind to their options for upward mobility, whereas security can help open their eyes to the possibilities ahead for success and independence. *Security is the inner food your clients need to live and thrive.*

If your client's greatest need is a sense of security, how do you help them know that security when it feels like you're facing monumental limits? The first step is to honestly assess whether those limits are perceived or real. As you work with her, some questions that will help her acknowledge her limits and face them courageously are:

- What limits is she facing?
- Which limits are internal and which are external?
- Which limits have been placed on her by others and which ones did she put on herself?
- What is one resource or action she can take to face her limitations with courage?

In the next chapter, we'll examine how your choices can impact her transformation from a person without hope to an independent woman.

A Real-Life Independent Woman

Mitzi Harris, Executive Director of Project Celebration
(Many, LA)

Though I've had the privilege of knowing Mitzi Harris only for a short time, I've been in awe of her organization's work for years. She is the executive director of Project Celebration, a nonprofit that serves survivors of domestic abuse and sexual assault in northwestern Louisiana. She first started with Project Celebration as an outreach advocate but rose to executive director 12 years ago. During her time with Project Celebration, Mitzi has helped grow them from two parishes into seven.

When I asked Mitzi to share some of the limiting beliefs she sees in her clients, she pointed out that low self-esteem was common among many of them. "They've never been allowed to work; 90% have been at home raising babies, doing housework and doing exactly what their partner tells them to do. Even if she did work, he's keeping tabs on her and her mileage. By the time they come to our office, their self-esteem is so depleted I don't know how they made it there." Thankfully, Mitzi ensures these women find support, shelter, education and a place to tell their stories.

As Mitzi's role has evolved into one that requires less one-on-one time with clients, she still makes time to go into the vestibule and let each client know just how big of a step it was and how strong they had to be just to get up and get dressed that day and make it on time to the program. Mitzi knows "the bruises will go away, but the mental abuse that has been instilled over and over again is so much harder to get past than something broken." Each day, she speaks words of life into women, hoping they will one day "become who they really are."

Mitzi, you're a true Independent Woman, helping other women see their potential to be one, too.

STEP TWO

Seeing Your Choices

*T*he first time I was forced to "see my choices" in life was when my children's father said he wanted a divorce. We were living on 238 acres that we had bought with the help of my father, Charles T. Beaird, out in the country. My husband had been brought up with horses and wanted to have a place to raise a few and give the children a chance at the lifestyle he had loved as a kid. Well ... that was okay with me until he left, leaving me with three small children and no means of support.

My children (Leslie, Trey, and Ben) and me by the lake at Lickskillet Plantation.

Needless to say, I was thrust into survival mode. I could sell the farm, but probably at a severe loss. I could raise cows, but I hated cows. I could farm mushrooms, but I didn't know a thing about growing them. So, after much ruminating, I decided the Thoroughbred horse business was the most feasible.

My father-in-law, Claude McCormick, master of the Oak Grove Hunt Club.

At that point, my only experience with horses was summer camp riding lessons in fourth grade and my father-in-law teaching me to jump fences so I could ride behind the hounds in the local hunt club where he was the master. The horses we rode at the hunt club were warmbloods, not thoroughbreds. In contrast to the warmbloods, the thoroughbreds were much more delicate, refined-looking, and higher-strung but were very intelligent. I quickly learned another significant difference between thoroughbreds and other horse breeds was that artificial breeding was forbidden in the Thoroughbred industry. A very strict registry held by the United States Jockey Club detailed each bloodline and its racing history. Because I liked the foals and mares, I decided to buy Thoroughbred broodmares in foal and sell the babies for profit for my new business—Lickskillet Plantation.

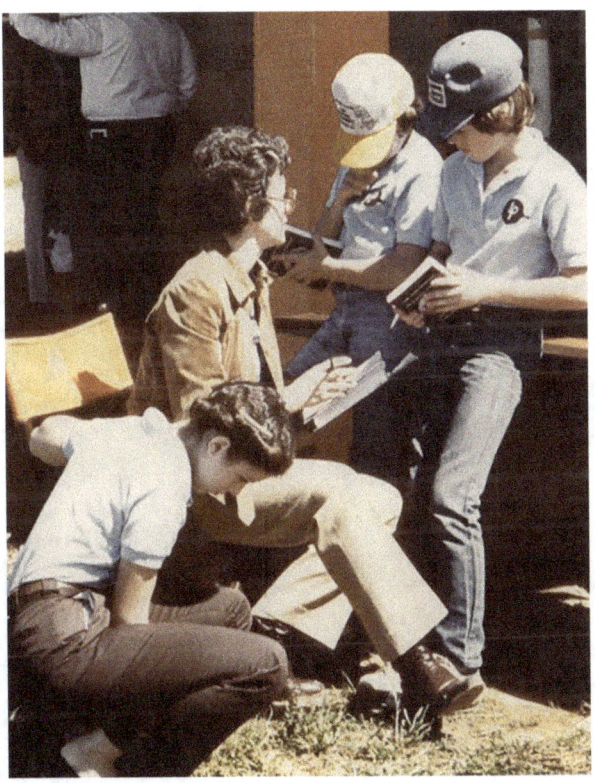

My three children helping me look for mares at Keeneland Sales, an auction house in Lexington, KY.

Papa (as I came to call Daddy after growing up) was on the board of Lickskillet Plantation. I thought his innate ability to look down a long column of figures and pick out the inaccurate one was a skill I could learn. I just knew that his "schooling" in budgets, profit and loss sheets, and cash flows would eventually seep into my bones or at least into my head. If I could just get all those numbers in all those little cells on those green 8.5x14 sheets to add up to the correct answers, Lickskillet Plantation and I would be set! Though Papa's fiscal teachings caused me angst every month, they were also highly prized.

Papa and me sitting in the sales arena at Keeneland in Lexington, KY, preparing to bid on broodmares.

Here I'm feeling the horse's leg to make sure there is no heat to indicate inflammation.

While the financial side of the business didn't come easily to me, my mother, Carolyn W. Beaird, was a tremendous support. Her devotion to my efforts and love of babies of all kinds gave me the confidence I needed to keep trying. Each time the latest Lickskillet Plantation Thoroughbred foal was born, Mother would drive 35 minutes in the middle of the night or right before dawn, with fine champagne in hand, to celebrate with me. In the 10 years I ran the plantation, we, amazingly enough, never had a single stillbirth. There wasn't one foal my manager and I weren't able to get out of the birth canal. Determined not to lose a single mare or foal, I even went to Fort Collins, Colorado, with a total of *zero* veterinary training, to learn how to palpate a mare.

This mare is Loire with her first foal, and the barn cat Tiger with her litter of kittens.

I wanted to learn everything I could to help those mares. As a mare would go into foaling (labor), Mom and I would stand in the barn with my farm manager and watch intently as that heaving mare finally got down on her side. She'd then slowly push that baby, hopefully headfirst, onto the soft bed we had made for them out of sweet timothy hay. Sometimes, the mare needed a little help, but more often, a whinnying little one struggled a minute and then rose to its wobbly feet and started searching for that life-giving nipple thanks to a nosey nudge from its mama. This was the most precious part for me—not only that Mother cared enough to drive all that way to be with me, but in doing so, saluted my efforts. She came to be with me and celebrate, to stand with me and beside me and to honor me for the work that I was doing. As mentioned, she loved all babies, and those little foals, along with the kittens our barn cat, Tiger, occasionally had in those same stalls, were no different.

Louisiana had a thriving Thoroughbred breeding program with Louisiana Downs located across the river in Bossier City, built to complement the older racetracks in the south of the state. Thanks to these developments and my Louisiana Thoroughbred owner friend Mason Grasty's introductions, I came to know several experienced horsemen around the state. Because I was so green at managing this kind of business, Mason recommended that I get my specific guidance from "the horse's mouth," so to speak, Lexington, Kentucky—the heart of the Thoroughbred business in this country. In Lexington, he introduced me to my first real mentor—John Bell of Jonabell Farm. As I arrived at Jonabell, John and his staff welcomed me with open arms. There, I met John's right-hand person, Sally Sharp, who eventually became a lifelong friend and confidante. She'd even invited me to stay at her precious little house in the historic district of Lexington when I went up to buy brood-mares or occasionally sell weanlings (foals at least a year old). At Jonabell, John graciously introduced me to his accountant, who taught me the financial side of things, even suggesting a particular computer program used in the industry. I was very young, but I didn't let that stop me—even if I was sitting next to the famous oil tycoon and Thoroughbred breeder H. L. Hunt or down the row from Penny Tweedy, the owner of the legendary Secretariat. As my mother would say, I was in tall cotton, but I was having a ball and learning every day. I put my all into my business, sometimes to the detriment of my children, like forgetting to pick up my youngest, Ben, from school or missing one of his siblings' events because I was out at the racetrack. But somehow, despite my women-belong-at-home upbringing, it never occurred to me that I shouldn't be doing this or that I couldn't at least try to make the business a success.

Moneywise, the plantation turned out to be a complete bust; healthwise, it was also a disaster thanks to a peptic ulcer. But, like Penny, I made inroads for women in Louisiana's Thoroughbred market and sold some mighty fine foals a few times. That September, with mentors like John and his staff in place, I set out to buy my first group of Thoroughbred broodmares at the Keeneland Sale, the global marketplace for Thoroughbred yearlings in Lexington. That weekend, I purchased eight broodmares and arranged for them to be sent home to Lickskillet Plantation.

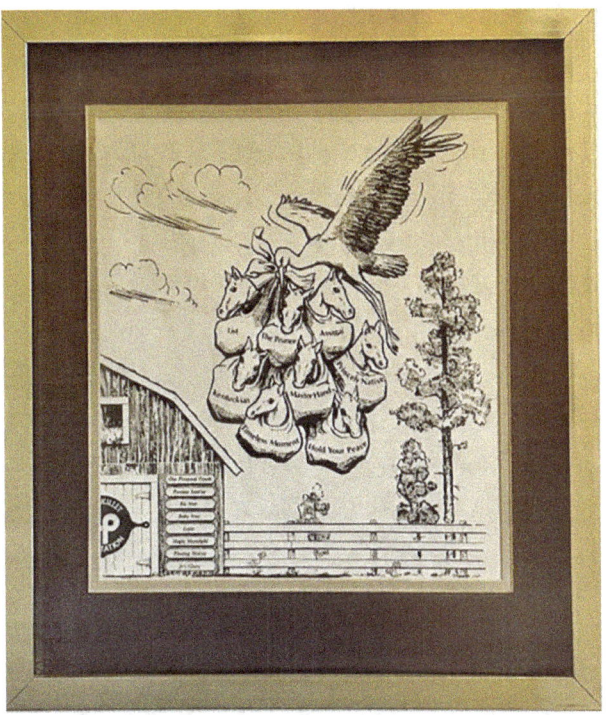

This is the drawing my brother John Beaird had made for me to commemorate my first crop of foals born at Lickskillet Plantation. The mares' names are on the barn and the names of the studs are on the stork sacks.

Being in debt up to my eyeballs from the mortgage of my land left me with a raging ulcer from the stress. But counter to common sense, I pressed onward and upward. I didn't know it yet, but this would be my path for the next 10 years.

Several years into this venture, I topped the Louisiana Breeders Weanling Sale! Having my babies sell at the highest price put me on the radar of Louisiana's top horsemen. Seeing that I must be doing something right, they brought me on as the first woman to serve on the Louisiana Thoroughbred

Breeders Association board. These two events should have been significant milestones in my journey to recognizing myself as an independent woman, but alas, that reckoning was yet to be. Sadly, with the severe downturn in the oil business in the '80s, the Thoroughbred business tanked. The price of horses had risen considerably when the Saudis entered the game internationally. However, when the price of the oil that provided their wealth began to drop, they left the Thoroughbred market, causing sale prices to drop dramatically. The trickle-down effect forced me to bail out of the business entirely and say goodbye to Lickskillet Plantation and my beloved mares. Amazingly, my ulcer disappeared with my loss of stress, so there was some saving grace—the restoration of my health.

This is a view of the front pasture of Lickskillet Plantation with the first year's mares and foals enjoying the green grass.

Running the business taught me several lessons. First and foremost, I learned that I, a woman, could indeed make it in a man's world. The only other woman Thoroughbred breeder I knew then was Penny Tweedy, who had raised, raced, and stood Secretariat at stud (mares' owners paid handsomely to be bred to him)! I had for sure been in tall cotton. But I had also made a name for myself in the Louisiana market and, for several years, continued to receive checks in the mail every time one of the foals I had bred and sold won a Louisiana race. Having my efforts recognized by my peers, combined with the skills I'd gained breeding and selling thoroughbreds, led to a growing sense of confidence and affirmed my place as a business leader. Later, that would propel me to start a nonprofit business training women on how to make it big in "a man's world."

Secondly, Lickskillet also taught me how to run a business. Nonprofits, much to many founders' chagrin, must, in many ways, be run like any other business to survive. *Accounting* skills are essential in a nonprofit business and can be invaluable when mastering the skill of *fundraising*, a process similar to *raising capital* in a for-profit business. A nonprofit's mission and purpose always drive it, but a strong fiscal underpinning must guide these efforts. Unlike a for-profit business, with a nonprofit, the net after expenses goes back into the business rather than into the owner's pocket. *Leadership* is another transferable and necessary skill, whether directed at paid or volunteer staff. Additionally, *community networking* is like *finding buyers* for your product or service in the for-profit field. The skills you've learned as an executive director are part of what makes you an independent woman, but you first have to recognize that expertise. Like me, you're probably often unaware of your abilities. Start by looking at your motivation for being in this field in order to see how your skills developed from your passions. Did you start on the street, get help, and want to give back? Did you work in a nonprofit program and fall in love with the work and the clients you served but found yourself wanting to do more? Or did you want to make more money to do a better job of sustaining your family? Even though people in this field are seriously underpaid for the effort and time they put in, it's a steady income, and changing lives beats slinging hamburgers, right? Whatever the reason behind your decision to lead a nonprofit, you've taken the bull by the horns and deserve a great deal of recognition and backing for doing so.

The Key to Inner Transformation: Self-Worth

One of the most powerful tools I've come to wield over the years is the understanding that choices don't merely lead to change—they can also lead to an inner transformation. Fortunately, your metamorphosis process doesn't have to take nearly as long as mine. It all begins in the mind with reframing your thoughts. Reframing can move you from feeling hopeless to seeing the many possibilities on the horizon. With this perspective, you can make the best choice for what your vision of being an independent woman looks like. I shared earlier that there were many things I could have done with those 238 acres. I saw many choices and ultimately decided to follow through with what seemed to make the most sense at the time. It paid off, figuratively in my learnings and to some degree literally, with those residual checks. But most importantly, it also led to my inner transformation—I was starting to see that, like you, I was an independent woman.

My inner transformation started with reframing my thoughts around my self-worth. As the author of the *Self-Love Workbook for Women* Megan Logan says: "By releasing self-doubt, we become free to fill up that space with self-worth."[9] Instead of being told who I was or could be when my husband left, I chose to gather the tools I needed to increase my confidence on the inside—tools like acknowledging my unique talents and strengths, practicing positive self-talk, and making a concerted effort to love and appreciate myself as I was.

By recognizing that I'd already done things that proved I could, I propelled myself into the little engine that could. Not to say it was easy, but I've learned that women can do anything they set their minds to if they just get out of their own way and try, try, try!

Positive self-talk is a tricky one. For years, well-meaning authors tried to teach me to quit listening to the negative voice in my head and replace it with a positive one. Well, that's fine and dandy, but if you're like me and those positive thoughts are about as foreign to you as Greek, you're up a creek without a paddle. I must admit that it wasn't until I heard positive words about me come out of the mouths of trusted friends that I began to believe that some of what they were saying might be true. Over time, I even learned to ask for these truths from people I knew wouldn't simply tell me what I wanted to hear but saw my potential for independent woman status. Slowly, I was able to occasionally shut that negative voice up when she started berating me about whatever I shouldn't be doing, or how fat I was, or that I wasn't doing anything worthwhile with my life. Now that last lie was a real bugger. It wasn't until I recognized real accomplishments that I could no longer discount that I finally let that lie go. My transformation wasn't overnight, but it was gradual, and my progress continued with each year that passed.

These are my besties, from left to right: Sharon Spurlin, Sally Gorrell, Molly Seeligson, and me! I rely on them for the whole truth and nothing but the truth.

As you work on your inner transformation, be patient with yourself. Reach out and seek that untainted opinion from people you trust, especially women who have known and loved you for a while. Don't only ask for advice about what you're doing wrong but also about what you're doing right! While you may not be able to see how far you come in your journey, I suspect your friends will. As for your clients, the message is the same. As poet Rupi Kaur said, "How you love yourself is how to teach others to love you." Always lead others with this in mind.

I recently rediscovered a book given to me by my high school buddies with inscriptions in the back. Not only had I forgotten the gift, but I certainly didn't remember that my friends had inscribed it back in the 1950s. The book was a true treasure with unsolicited affirmations.

Self-Esteem

When I say that I started my inner transformation journey addressing my self-worth, I did that because I had to understand my value as a person (self-worth) before I could recognize the value in my accomplishments (self-esteem).[10] Low self-esteem is perhaps the most defining attitude of mentally abused women. In my case, it's something I'll probably wrestle with forever to a degree, but I'm certainly much more self-assured now than as that little girl in grade school. When we wrestle with low self-esteem, it leads to feeling overwhelmed, inadequate, and immobilized. If we stay frozen, comparing ourselves to everyone else, we eventually give up. We stop fighting. We lose our chance to make things better for ourselves or our families. On the other hand, if we have high self-esteem, we see ourselves as competent and able to face life's challenges.

When I think of how my self-esteem evolved, I partly owe it to the special love of my mother's parents, my only grandparents—Mr. B and Argie. They gave me that "you're special" sense of love. My granddaddy, B, made me feel that way every time I was with him, whether we were "wetting" a hook, sitting in rocking chairs on the front porch looking at the lake, or hanging out behind the batter's box at a baseball game on a school night. He was always present and supportive despite the vast difference in our ages. With the gentleness of a kitten, Mr. B taught me how to drive a car. He and my grandmother, Argie, were my refuge even if she didn't have his sense of humor or soft nature. She taught me how to type, sew, and play solitaire with a vengeance. Sometimes, she'd even place her "lucky" white linen handkerchief on her head, hoping it would help her best me at her favorite card game.

Of all my memories with B and Argie, my fondest is getting in the queen-sized bed in their guest room. They would pull the curtains and crank up the window unit air conditioner until it blew at "cold" speed. Perhaps the best naps I ever took were in that bed with the lightweight comforter pulled up to my chin and my head nestled into their feather-soft pillow. After church on Sundays, I could always find Argie standing in her little kitchen over a huge cast iron skillet full of fried chicken. Then, the seven of us would sit in the dining room for a scrumptious lunch of fried chicken, collard greens cooked with ham hock, of course, and string beans (from B's backyard or lake garden) that I'd helped string. As if that wasn't a feast in and of itself, Sunday lunch would also always have fresh ripe tomatoes in season with corn on the cob or black-eyed peas with okra and tomatoes. I don't think I've ever tasted a tomato as good as those since. Mr. B grew many varieties and knew the names of them all. For dessert, we'd have pie or figs that Argie and I picked off a huge fig tree in their backyard.

While Mr. B or Argie may not have sat me down with a book of positive affirmations about self-esteem, they did something even better: they showed me my value time and again with their behavior. Improving self-esteem requires changes in two areas: behavior and thought patterns. Though their love was life-changing to my young heart, my thoughts were often negative. If I was going to feel more positive about myself, I needed to replace those negative ones with more positivity. As Elizabeth Gilbert wrote in *Eat, Pray, Love*, "You need to learn how to select your thoughts just the same way you select your clothes every day. This is a power you can cultivate."[11]

I once visited an executive director in eastern Colorado who told me of a client trapped in a toxic marriage. Not only would the woman's husband not allow her to have a checking account, but he wouldn't even let her visit the bank holding THEIR money. The husband's deplorable behavior took the phrase "being pushed around" to new heights. Hearing this woman's story showed me how rough it can be for some wives but also how change is possible, even for those abused, *if* they can learn what they are capable of. In this woman's case, she reached out for help—that was her behavior change. Through support from a nonprofit organization, she gained positive reinforcement to change her thought patterns and, in time, her self-esteem.

If you're struggling to change your thought patterns, part of the problem may be a lack of compassion for yourself. Imagine saying, "You aren't worth anything! You can't do anything right!" to your niece, child, or grandchild. You wouldn't even consider it, right? Of course not! Yet, how often do we talk about ourselves this way? Imagine how destructive those words are to that little girl inside you! She's caring, worthwhile, and hard-working, and deserves recognition for her abilities ... even those skills she hasn't mastered yet. She needs and deserves all the RAH RAH you can give her.

Seeing the potential choices available to you requires replacing the dark, negative inner words to allow the light of truth—what you could be—to become visible. What changes can you make in your day-to-day life to be more productive, happier, and self-assured? Who can you ask for an unbiased opinion of your gifts, talents, and skills? Don't forget that many of the older, more experienced executive directors in your community are excellent resources and are usually more than willing to help you see yourself from another perspective.

The Client Path

If you've seen your worth, begin passing on your knowledge—even if it's through telling your own story as you've seen me do here. As I mentioned previously, it only takes one person to shine a light on our possibilities for transformation. Often, the very program these clients are engaged in offers them the skills that will enable them to get a job or a better-paying one, which can be their ticket to independence or some measure of sustainability. There are even programs out there like WINcome, supported by the Women's Foundation of Colorado, that offer stipends to help women get back on their feet. With a strong self-worth, a boost of self-esteem, and the right kind of support and knowledge, the sky's the limit!

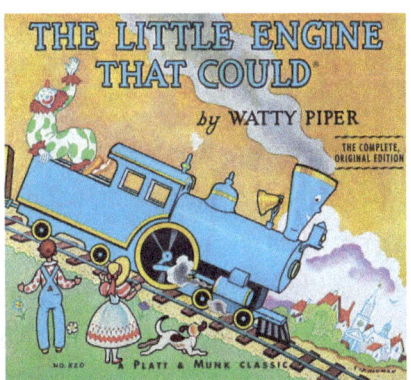

To mentor your clients, you may lead them on potential stepping stones to future career choices they see as possible. These stepping stones might be such things as more training in a field that they feel drawn to, more education, and more focus on helping them understand that they are unique, worthwhile, and important. Their passions must eventually guide them, and these may start as pie in the sky, but with your help, they can become a reality. As you dig deep together to imagine what choices are possible for themselves and their family, they'll slowly understand that, like the independent women they are, they, too, can be the author of their independence. They, too, can be the little engine that could.

A Real-Life Independent Woman
Dr. Sharon Green, Executive Director of Oasis of Hope (Shreveport, LA)

Dr. Sharon Green, executive director of Oasis of Hope, works with women in STEM (science, technology, engineering, and math) fields, and I'm privileged to call her a friend. During our interview, she told me my major limitation is funding. So I have learned to bring in partners and collaborators. "I know there's no sense in reinventing the wheel," she says.

"In order to be really good at serving people, it takes introspection … or self-awareness. You've definitely got to be called to it. Yes, being called helps with burnout. I have to pull away at times and make sure that I sleep enough, eat when I should, and am nurtured in whatever way is right for me. Also, surrounding myself with people who've done it and who care about me," says Sharon. I have had years and years of counseling and yet I'm not always not prepared to deal with the issues that come up. "But what I can do," Sharon continues, "is be an active and effective listener. I'm not going to leave my women stranded. By using good ole gut-level common sense when I feel inadequate, I just listen until something comes up," she says.

"It's about making a difference in the lives of the people we serve," Sharon advises. She often encourages the girls she works with to dream about where they want to go. Once they have a dream in mind, she asks them to determine what they must stop doing to reach their dreams.

When it comes to the mental obstacles she sees her clients facing, she's seen firsthand the damage done by "shrinking" or putting themselves down. Her goal is to help clients step into their own sense of confidence so their belief in themselves doesn't rely on what others think. Needless to say, that process is much easier when a client understands her full destiny and purpose. Once she can see her possibilities, she and Dr. Green discuss what skills or training she needs to move ahead. This step-by-step process allows clients to begin seeing themselves as capable of reaching their aspirations, taking dreams from mere fantasies to tangible goals they can work toward.

STEP THREE

Owning Your Abilities

$\mathcal{E}$arly in my adult life, my father asked me to be a director of the family foundation he and Mother founded, the Charles T. and Carolyn W. Beaird Family Foundation. Papa, the foundation's president, insisted that the foundation exist into perpetuity, so he brought me, my younger sister, and brother into the organization. He and Mother were equally committed to keeping the family close and educated about philanthropy far into the future. Every summer, we gather with all the family members 18 and older who've chosen to join the member board. While we get down to business, the younger siblings enjoy time with their cousins. The two-day event is filled with continuing education about how a foundation works, celebrations of the grants given over the past year, and long-overdue catch-ups on our lives, now spanning from coast to coast. Since most of the foundation's grants are based in Shreveport, Louisiana and the surrounding parishes, and very few of us live there, this allows us to stay connected to each other as well as to the historical roots of the organization.

Acting as one of the directors of the Charles T. and Carolyn W. Beaird Family Foundation gave me invaluable experience in board service and the process a foundation goes through to help fund nonprofit organizations. Papa taught my siblings and me how to read a profit and loss sheet, a balance sheet, and a budget and how they differentiated. Each year, Mama and Papa presented us with a selection of submitted grants, and my siblings and I got to participate in choosing which would be funded. To select a candidate, we had to understand the grantee's budget, their proposed use of this money, and the probable success or failure of the program they were offering. We even had to examine the strength of the potential grantee's board of directors, the leadership of the program (usually an executive director), and whether the mission fit into their budget constraints. We also had to decide if the applicant fit into the mission of our Foundation: "The Carolyn W. and Charles T. Beaird Family Foundation is committed to improving the Shreveport and Bossier City region of Louisiana through assisting organizations to add opportunity, freedom of action and choice, self-betterment and a climate for change to the lives of the people they serve." To this day, these skills are the most treasured from my early life. Little did I know then, but they were to be the groundwork for my lifelong passion to teach women how to become independent women.

Another central teaching from that period came from watching my mother's volunteer work and seeing how a small amount of money or a little time could change someone's life. Though Mama deferred to my father in almost every area, this was the arena in which she soared on her own. Once, a friend of Mother's decided to start a track team for underserved children. Naturally, the first thing the track team needed was shoes. Mama couldn't get to the store fast enough. She did a similar thing when the brand-new neonatal center at the public hospital said it was vital for premature babies to be held as much as possible. (When I was a preemie, mothers could only stand by the bassinet, so habitually holding newborns was a new concept.) Once again, Mama couldn't wait to get those much-needed rocking chairs delivered. Thanks to Mama's big heart, I was introduced to the volunteer world, an essential element of most small nonprofits and often the majority of their staff. But because my mother was a stay-at-home mom, I failed to recognize her work as the career it could be or the skills she had as the valuable tools I'd need to make it in the nonprofit world down the road.

The family foundation's "support staff" at one of our membership meetings.

The office for the programs that were run for the families in Ledbetter Heights.

During my time as president of my family's foundation, I was active in our project in Ledbetter Heights, formerly called "The Bottoms," in Shreveport, LA. We thought that if we remodeled the "shotgun" homes in this neighborhood, people would return and revive it. But after 20 years of these efforts, we realized that the community would forever see these homes as "slave quarters" and, therefore, not desirable, so we ultimately gave all our houses to the city. During this period, I gained lots of insight and experience in low-income neighborhoods, even though our efforts to completely revive the neighborhood had failed. I spent many afternoons handing out candy and balls to little kids while the executives running the programs we were funding gave mothers desperately needed advice on how to survive. Over those two decades, I gradually came to understand how poverty and isolation affect people. Mothers were struggling to make it on their own with low-level jobs, barely aware of much outside of their small neighborhood despite the downtown commercial district being practically in their backyard. These moms had been in such a survival mode that they weren't aware help was essentially next door. Something shifted once these women learned about the social service programs that we and other funders in the area were backing—programs that offered much-needed training and financial assistance. Suddenly, a chance at a higher-paying job, better housing, and something close to security was no longer a pipe dream. It could be their reality.

Here I am, hosting a party I threw on my birthday for those precious Ledbetter Heights kids, hoping to give them some treats, gifts, and plenty of fun.

To be perfectly honest, it was years before I truly acknowledged the usefulness and power of the skills and insight I was gaining. But because I had been up close and personal with many of these families, I came to understand how their isolation and lack of knowledge of the help they were entitled to kept them from imagining a better life, much less a future in a job they were not only passionate about but one that paid them a living wage.

Harnessing Our Power

As women, our equanimity empowers us to embrace our strength and power to seek what's most important to us. It gives us the confidence to own our abilities, skills, and accomplishments, no matter how modest. Life is too short to spend on anything that doesn't fill us with passion and make us feel alive. Putting our innate abilities into action gives us purpose in getting up in the morning. It's the kind of "work" we want to talk about after a long day, whether calling our best friend on the drive home or filling our partner in on our day over pillow talk. As Brené Brown says, "We all have gifts and talents. When we cultivate those gifts and share them with the world, we create a sense of meaning and purpose in our lives."[12]

So, "What are my skills?" you may ask.

1. **Leader:** The first skill you possess is leadership, whether it's around your subordinates, your clients, your board, or your community. Perhaps you have staff or volunteers who help you carry out the day-to-day of your program,

but even if you don't, you still must mentor your clients. In both cases, leadership is paramount and taken for granted because it comes with the job. As the executive director, you also select and lead the nonprofit's board of directors. Your board is key to your nonprofit's support in the community and, ultimately, its sustainability. After all, your board holds the last word regarding fiscal and legal problems, so if they don't know how to support you … Houston, we have a problem.

2. **Strategic Planner:** A second skill you possess as an executive director is your ability to implement both long and short-term goals with strategic, tactical decisions that align with your mission. As Erik Hanberg notes in *The Little Book of Nonprofit Leadership: an Executive Director's Handbook for Small (and Very Small) Nonprofits*, "The board may set guidelines, define policies and balance the budget, but, ultimately, the operational decisions are up to you as the executive director."[13] As the executive director, you lead the charge for building and fostering community partnerships and securing additional funding so your nonprofit can grow.

3. **Manager:** Another skill you possess is the ability to manage the program, the clients and the budget. Again, there may be others to help you juggle all these hats, but *you* are the main "man" deciding what training is necessary for the multi-pronged outcomes your clients are seeking. In creating a job training program for your clients, for instance, you understand that the program

must include skills like dressing for the job they want, the importance of dependability, and how vital it is to be on time.

4. **Financial Wizard and Grant Guru:** The financial aspect of being an executive director is also multi-pronged. It involves designing the budget, ensuring it's adhered to and, most importantly, helping raise the money necessary to fund it. There are capacity-building courses to learn these skills, but you must master them for the program's sustainability. Lastly, you must either become proficient at writing grants to fund the majority of the program or hire someone who is.

If you're the founder of the nonprofit, these managerial, operational, financial, and leadership skills are in addition to the courage and self-belief it took to form the nonprofit in the first place. You had to have the vision, passion, and sometimes fiscal resources to get a nonprofit off the ground—that's no small feat!

Hubs: A One-Stop Shop

There are nonprofit organizations that offer counseling to "just get away from abuse," ones for job training, some to help clients find affordable housing and others ("hubs") that offer all those services in one place. Thankfully, one-stop hubs that house multiple programs so women can get all the necessary resources are becoming more commonplace. Can you imagine if you had to take three buses just to get the children situated and then another bus to reach your job training for the day, only to repeat the process to get back home? Golly, the amount of effort and perseverance that would take! Like so many of these women, I, for one, would probably give up. This potential obstacle is why many nonprofits have wised up and started grouping these programs.

Hubs are an innovative way for nonprofits with similar client bases to band together and offer a wide range of programs. Together, these organizations can share the rent, utilities, phone and internet lines, parking, and security. Since they are in the same building and share resources, they can also network easily. That way, when a client comes to one place for her program, she'll see other possibilities, maybe even a daycare, to cut down on her transportation nightmare.

The Client Path

Now that you have all these incredible skills, how do you pass them on to your clients? One subtle way of mentoring your clients is pointing out the parallels between their mastery of everyday skills like housekeeping, caring for their kids, and getting to the program on time and how they coincide with the learned skills necessary for success in the job market. An executive director does this kind of counseling easily and naturally while operating her program.

Imagine that you happen to be waiting in the lobby when a woman we'll call Genevieve comes through the door in an ill-fitting dress, tennis shoes, and a tattered handbag overflowing with baby items and emergency peanut butter crackers (my mother was never without those crackers). Her face is one big question mark, her eyes filled with fear that she can't afford the services you offer. She'd wanted to make this move for months but couldn't muster enough courage until her husband called her a useless burden on the family over breakfast that morning. She was tired of hearing that she wasn't pretty enough or thin enough and that her cooking stunk. Tired of being told she's a bad mother because he wants to nap in "*his*" chair in front of the TV, but the kids won't stop crying. Tired of being told she's not smart enough to get a job because she didn't finish high school. Of course, he didn't graduate either, but his welding job was putting food on the table and she should be grateful. Every bit of her insecurity is visible on her face and in her wobbly gait as she comes through the door, looking around for who's in charge. Still, she's decided to see if this financial beginning is possible, as the kind lady at the YWCA said it was.

As she comes in the door, you stand to greet her and offer her a chair to sit across from you on the other side of the small reception room. You ask all the necessary questions before inviting her to come with you to meet the volunteers and other participants who are already working in the next room. You must ensure that all her questions get answered truthfully but with deep congratulations on how wonderful it is that she's here. You fully understand how hard it was for her to take that step, so you assure her that it will get easier each time and that, if she's willing to continue to show up, she will begin to see new possibilities for her future. You encourage her to talk with the other participants about their experiences and to lean on the volunteers and staff for whatever she needs. No question is stupid; even if the staff has no immediate answer, they will work to get one for her. As you show her around and explain the programs you offer, you share some of your story, hoping it will boost her confidence. "When I first came here, I too had doubts about my ability to succeed. But over the last two years, I've learned a lot, reached out for help a lot, and failed a lot. But I'm still here and loving it even more than when I first came through that very door. It's my desire to, in some small way, give back for all the help I've been given along the way. Hopefully, in a month or two, you'll feel this empowered, too, Genevieve. But, if not, we'll help you find another road that may be a better fit for you!"

When you help women like Genevieve recognize that simply getting into your program demonstrates practical abilities they already possess, it reinforces their confidence in their current skills. Once these women see their skills (caretaker, time manager, multitasker, etc.) as transferable into the workforce, they'll understand that these abilities can be enhanced to take them into the better life they desire.

A Real-Life Independent Woman

Kate Horle, Executive Director of the Center for Work Education and Employment (CWEE) (Denver, CO)

Kate Horle, executive director of the Center for Work Education and Employment (CWEE), is a second-generation employee because her mother worked there as a coach. In her interview, she shared that social services work is hard. She says,

"We serve 1,200 families a year; 51% of those families are experiencing violence, often through domestic abuse. A significant portion of them are housing unstable, either homeless or living on somebody's couch. They are very hungry. Because this is exhausting work, we build a staff structure to address this, including every other Friday off and two weeks a year that we are closed for wellness."

Kate went on to talk about how her clients are worse off now than they were 20 years ago because of the increasing gap between the wealthy and families experiencing poverty. "We've built an economic system in this country that requires two parents to work to really subsist. There are no choices now for a single parent working if you don't have a family member you can leave your kiddos with. Childcare in Denver is $2,000 a month, so if you're making $40,000 a year, you pay more than half of that in childcare."

Kate continues, "I don't think people understand the skills you need to survive when you're living in poverty, like organization, logistics management, and time management. The discernment process is new to clients because they are mostly thinking, 'How do I feed my kids this week and how do I make sure my abuser isn't abusing me or my children?' You know, those are survival things. A big piece of the stabilization process is helping folks tap into who they are. What do they care about? Where does their passion lie? What's important to them? We also work closely with employers willing to do skills-based hiring, not just education-based hiring. Often, folks have been working in an industry because it was available to them, not because they care about it. And they're not successful. So, there is a lot of conversation with them to understand what really matters to them and what really drives them."

STEP FOUR

Letting Your Passions Guide You

*O*n a somber day in March, at the end of a year-long road serving as the scheduler for my brother-in-law's unsuccessful race for the U.S. Senate in Colorado, I received a call that forever altered my path. Having spent years putting out political flyers for the candidates my father endorsed and my learnings as a political science major in college, politics was in my blood. Perhaps, at the time, some small part of me even thought politics was part of my future calling. But, that day, as I answered the phone only to hear my friend Sue Damour, the executive director of The Women's Foundation of Colorado (WFCO), on the other end of the line, I had no inkling that life was about to reveal that my truest passions lay far outside politics. "Susan, if you're interested, I have a job for you!" Sue practically sang through the phone line. "It pays about what you're making now (of course, that's nothing!)" She laughed. "But you'd be working with a woman whom I think you'll really like." The woman was called Letty Bass, and she had moved to Denver from Dallas several years before.

Within a week of Sue's call, I arrived at the Denver offices of WFCO, ready to start a new and, unbeknownst to me, final chapter on my journey to finding my lifelong work. So why did I accept this job when I could have easily packed up and returned to Dallas instead? First, I'd fallen in love with Denver and wanted to stay. Next, I knew Sue well and trusted her instincts regarding my abilities and personality being a good fit for the foundation. Lastly, I accepted the job because my time with the Beaird Family Foundation had shown me that this was an arena in which I was comfortable, knowledgeable, and passionate. WFCO specifically worked with nonprofits that served women, and by then, I knew that the independence of women was *my thing*! (If you haven't already done so, check out my website: independentwomen.net.)

Women's Home Improvement

I learned a lot about how to run a business from my father, but my mother's volunteer work in nonprofits turned out to be the best fit for me. I quickly learned that for a nonprofit to stay afloat, it had to run like a business where the mission's success depended on how well it worked for its participants, not on how much money it put in the owner's pocket. A nonprofit's emphasis is on serving others wherever their needs are, whether it's job training, housing, addiction relief, or simple education. The passion in the nonprofit world may be just as strong as that of the for-profit entrepreneurs, but it's motivated by entirely different values and goals.

Would you believe me if I told you that nonprofits are responsible for 12.8 million jobs? That's nearly 10% of the U.S. employment![14] In her book *Guide to Nonprofit Leadership*, nonprofit superhero Joan Garry said nonprofits "represent the third-largest workforce behind retail and food. ... Nonprofits are responsible for more jobs than American manufacturing.

In addition to all the good nonprofits do to fix our broken world, this sector is a key driver of our economy." In 2022 alone, nonprofits contributed $1.4 trillion to the U.S. economy—a whopping 5.2% of our Gross Domestic Product.[15] So, as Garry would say, "When we say nonprofits matter, we are not kidding around."[16]

After witnessing the undeniable impact of the state's nonprofits firsthand through WFCO, I knew it was time to collaborate. If we could make this big of an impact individually, how much more could we accomplish together? How many jobs could we help fill or even create? After several years of training under Letty and others at WFCO, she and I decided it was time to bring some of the state's best nonprofits together for a day-long retreat. Our aim was twofold: 1) to allow the nonprofits to network and learn from each other and 2) to see where our services overlapped and spot any program gaps that needed to be filled in Colorado. These women spent the day networking and sharing their successes, failures, and best practices in how to do their jobs. The event was a success, clarifying what programs were valuable for our clients and showing us that nontraditional training for women was missing. Fields like construction, plumbing, electrical, carpentry, tiling, and painting were beginning to open to women, and we wanted our clients to be able to take advantage of those high-paying jobs.

Within a few weeks, I was sure that my next job would be, by far, my biggest yet. It was time to say goodbye to my friends at the WFCO and start a nontraditional program for women right where I was in Colorado. My "big picture" mindset and familiarity with nonprofits and the funds necessary to sustain them gave me the impetus to start this new nonprofit, Women's Home Improvement (WHI). The program was my avenue to provide training for women who wanted a chance at independence. Since I didn't have a clue how to start a nonprofit from the ground up, I gathered friends and mentors to help guide me. To keep me motivated. I also designed a poster called my "dream board." It contained all my ideas, passions, hopes, and possible obstacles to my road to success. I kept this in front of me while making calls for funding, picking the brains of other executive directors, or just trying to figure out what should come next.

We met frequently over the next two years, finding the money, staff, and location (a Quonset hut in the predominantly Hispanic part of the city) to form WHI. I couldn't have accomplished this alone! While I may have had a general idea of the program I wanted to create, I didn't have any experience in the trades I wanted to offer training in, much less access to the local women working in them who we'd need to hire as teachers. I understood the monetary requirements, but I knew it would take helpers to convince the friends and contacts I had made while working on the campaign to join up and strengthen our efforts. I hadn't been in Denver long enough to understand the real estate market enough to find a suitable location and building to house us, so I needed help! But with all of us working together, bouncing things off each other and taking advantage of individual connections and skills, the group coalesced into my board of directors, and soon we were advertising the program to funders as well as other programs that had women who would benefit from WHI's training.

Long before WHI began training women, we knew one thing—we would devote ourselves to recruiting, training, and assisting low-income women with nontraditional job skills and the independent attitudes they'd need for self-sufficiency. If we could provide the essentials of a real job experience, a résumé for a for-profit employer and the internal motivation they needed, they'd be well on their way to becoming self-sustaining independent women in the workforce.

Our initial plan looked something like this:

- The first class will have no more than 15 women.
- Instruction will take place in a convenient church or community center.
- We will find a retailer or manufacturer to supply the tools we need.
- Classes will meet four to five hours a day, four to five days a week, for at least six months.

- Education will be provided on minor electrical and plumbing modules; wall repair and painting; carpentry for repairing floors, doors, windows, trim; and the rudiments of large appliance troubleshooting.
- Additional training areas will include safety, sexual harassment prevention, remedial math, and some physical fitness.
- Classroom instruction will be enriched with on-site work with Habitat for Humanity and other local nonprofits.

As you might imagine, things didn't work out exactly as planned. For instance, we decided the most promising format was five days a week for six weeks. In hopes of getting the best possible teachers, I contacted the local carpentry, plumbing, and electrical unions and asked for tradeswomen willing to teach their skills. Since my program manager was an electrician, she planned the six-week program and put it into motion.

The first part of the course consisted of lessons in identifying barriers to getting and succeeding in a trades job and discussions of self-concept and self-esteem. A man who likes and values himself is typically viewed as confident and exhibiting a healthy self-interest. On the other hand, self-esteem in a woman is frequently condemned for being vain, arrogant, or conceited. At WHI, we wanted our women to believe in their inherent value so they could begin making things better for themselves and their communities. To succeed, they needed to see themselves as the powerful, creative, and worthwhile women they were. With that goal in mind, we led them through numerous exercises centered around positive self-worth and activities designed to improve their problem-solving and decision-making skills. We also taught them assertiveness—how to stand up for themselves without violating the rights of others. And, because this was nontraditional training, we also demonstrated how to deal with the various situations that arise when you're the only female on the job. Our ideal outcome for them was not to act passively but to work to build healthy relationships within these generally male-dominated environments.

The hands-on part of our training consisted of the participants making a small house within our 20-foot-high structure. First, they'd nail in the studs, then the rafters and then the drywall. Next, they'd wire the "home," carefully installing the plumbing so it wouldn't stop up or back up into our yard. By the time they finished, the structure looked like a backyard dollhouse. Then, they'd tear it all down to prepare it for the next class. Often, my manager incorporated tiling, painting, and other skill sets into the program as frequently as she could find the women to teach them.

I quickly learned that women are particularly good at electrical work because of their fine motor skills and attention to detail. I remember one graduate especially well, Debbie Osterholt. She was down on her luck, living with her four children in her car. But, after completing our six-week program, she got a job as an electrician on a state-run project for what today would be $26.33 per hour. Needless to say, she quickly moved her family into an apartment and returned to being a self-reliant member of society.

Women at work building their house in the Quonset hut.

This newspaper article features Women's Home Improvement graduate Debbie Osterholt.

Mount Massive

During my time building WHI, I enlisted in the year-long training program at Denver's Community Leadership Forum. My defining moment was during their four-day Outward Bound adventure in the "fourteeners"—the 53 14,000-foot-high mountains that grace Colorado's topography.[17] It's the sort of thing that, if you live there, you want to climb at least one in your lifetime. Many friends of mine climbed all 53 peaks each summer. Whew! Can you imagine?

This program had several parts besides the climb of Mount Massive. And, yes, that's the mountain's real name, thanks to it being the second-highest summit in Colorado.[18]

That's me in the back on the peak of Mount Massive.

This is the cliff where we learned to climb as well as rappel off with carefully trained guides.

During our training program, we spent one day learning how to rappel a 200-foot cliff used by the U.S. Marine Corps in their training. After that, we spent another day learning a rope game, then finishing our long day with a night alone in the wilderness. As we climbed the mountain from our base camp, the air became thinner and thinner, and breathing became harder, particularly with my asthmatic condition. Thankfully, our guide often reminded us to take not just small steps but TINY ones. Amazingly, this helped considerably, and although it took seven hours, we made it to the summit. As thrilled as I was by the view from the peak, I was even more proud of myself for the strength and tenacity it took to reach the summit. No one was more surprised than I that I was able to make the climb at 50 years old.

Our path up Mount Massive.

The 13 hours up and back down the mountain were demanding and scary because I didn't know how I would react to those heights or if my knees would hold up coming down. Much to my amazement, I walked across that snow-covered three-foot-wide peak with absolutely no fear of looking down, no more so than standing on the sidewalk in front of my house. In fact, when several other women panicked from being at that height on such a narrow path, I ended up helping them get across the peak so they could sign the document that proved they had made it to the top! After getting back to base camp, all I could think about was how wrong my father and classmates were to tell me I wasn't athletic. Until then, my only outdoor activities had been before the age of 12—playing house under the weeping willow tree with my next-door neighbor Nancy, hide and seek with my siblings, catching fireflies on a summer evening, or sitting at a drive-in movie. In my 30s, I took up tennis, later racquetball, and eventually pickleball in my 70s. See, you, too, can grow and change!

Once we recognize our actual abilities, it can be the catalyst to opening the door to exploring our passions and imagination. If things were completely different, what would we do with our lives? After conquering Mount Massive, my mental realization that I was not a "weenie" after all was another underlying reason I began to believe I could do anything I wanted. I like what writer and director Issa Rae says: "I don't like being limited. I want to be able to flex other muscles and see what else I can do."[19] Boy, do I wish I had learned to flex my muscles earlier in life!

Pinpointing Your Passion

Let's talk about your innate passion and the values that make those passions attractive to you. A value isn't a want, a fantasy, or a wish. It's a deep-seated belief that must be honored for you to *be yourself.* Ask yourself: "What would make me feel most like myself? What floats my boat, fills my heart, and pulls me forward despite all the risks, likely pitfalls, setbacks, and just plain failures?"

Your passion isn't something you can ignore for long because it's part of who you are—your essence. On the other hand, your values can help you keep that passion on track by helping you figure out what's worth pursuing and how you want to reach your dream. Being in tune with this part of yourself and forming your career and lifestyle accordingly is happiness personified.

So, set your goals to express your passions, and let those passions be fueled and guided by the values that define you.

As you're working to pinpoint your passions, ask yourself questions like, "What are my values and are they a good fit for the job I'm in? Do these values line up with my goals? Are my passions in life fulfilled in this job? Why or why not?" If your current job doesn't align with the passions closest to your heart, be honest with yourself. Is it time for a new adventure? Is there another job that would be a better fit for the values and passion that brought you to your current role? How could you help yourself and your organization by making a change? Sometimes, both can benefit, even if it means walking away.

My mother gave me this sign years ago, and it's been on my desk ever since.

The Client Path

The women who walk through your front door are seeking guidance on how to fix their lives and escape those incessant voices that say, "You can't, you aren't." Rarely are they aware that they have a passion for anything. They want to know what's on the menu today: the soup of love and support, the well-done steak of belonging, or the wine that will, for a minute, make them believe they are special and worthy of any grand occasion. They want to believe they can go anywhere their heart takes them, that adventure awaits them in the cool waters of a grotto, or maybe in the thick of the redwoods, or somewhere along a seashore with the waves washing in. They want to believe they can become more than they ever imagined, more than Mother or Father or Granny ever thought was possible. It's not until they're made aware of the skills they already possess added to the ones they're learning in the program that they can see into a different future. You or any of your program staff members can be the catalyst for this transformation by simply being your affirming, dependable selves.

While the experience your clients gain in your program will undoubtedly impact their lives, the continued guidance and moral support they find with you and your team are the keys to their transformation. Little by little, these women will glimpse a possible future, whether it's finishing their GED, going on to higher education, or simply applying for a job with future advancement. In any case, it's critical that they begin to see down the road, out of their current box, and into a life of financial and physical security. No matter their current home life, they now have options they formerly lacked. With their newfound sense of security and these options at their fingertips, they'll likely start to discover their passions. But, before they can act on their passions, they must first recognize that they deserve and are capable of much more than their present circumstances. Once this bulb lights up, they're free to dream and admit to what they want to do with their lives.

For 15 years, I served on the board of a small independent school in Eureka Springs, Arkansas named Clear Spring School. During this time, I learned a lot about how important questions are in a classroom setting and all the different ways to bring them up. Clear Spring's classrooms were just the right size for 10 to 12 students in each. Instead of sterile white environments, the walls were covered with pictures and illustrations. When I was little, I remember simply sitting at my desk and taking notes as the teacher talked. However, these kids were doing projects, reading to each other and engaging in lively discussions about whatever the current topic was. In addition to listening to what the teacher had to say, they looked at each topic from all sides and, in doing so, made conclusions on their own. Had the teacher decided to test them on the spot, they would have passed with flying colors because it was clear they truly understood the material. Instead of telling the students what she wanted them to learn, the teacher invited them into the discussion as part of the learning process. In educational circles, we call this multisensory learning—a mix of visual, kinesthetic, and auditory learning (the only type I experienced in school). I invite you to try this method in your program.

Begin by consistently asking your clients questions in enough ways and contexts to ensure you get your points across. You can ask questions like:

- Is there a hobby you used to love or a job you aspired to before it got buried under all the stress and anxiety?
- What cause or profession resonates with you deeply?
- What makes you excited to get up in the morning?
- What keeps you engaged no matter what else is happening around you?
- What do you dream about, even if you don't think it's possible for you, only others?

STEP FIVE

Building on Your Success

*I*n the late '90s, I started taking phone courses, or "tele-classes," from Coach University (Coach U) with three other friends. The new program's series of classes was designed to teach us how to be life coaches for personal and business issues. At 54, learning new skills that might open the door to a new career was exciting! Having wrapped up my work with WHI, I was back in my hometown helping look after my aging parents and I desperately needed something to challenge me.

After about a year and a half, I graduated from Coach U and began to try to acquire clients to build a business in life coaching. I called my new business Independent Women. With my degree from Coach U under my belt, I started meeting with clients over the phone to help them move on with their lives in whatever arena they felt was lacking. As a coach, I'd move only as fast as my clients were willing to go but also nudge them forward when I thought they were more capable than they could see. I was their mirror, showing them where they stood while projecting a vision of just how far I knew they could go. Once they decided what kind of work they felt best suited them, I provided options for how to get into that field and the training that it might take to get there. As they proceeded along this path, we discussed their God-given skills and how they could better care for themselves. If they wanted to take on the responsibility of nurturing others without doing damage to themselves, they had to learn to prioritize their physical and mental health.

While I worked to build my coaching business, I was still on the Beaird Family Foundation board. I'd also begun collaborating with our local Louisiana Association of Nonprofits (LANO) staff member, Kay Irby. Kay and I decided to apply to the Beaird Foundation for funds to pilot a program that would help select executive directors in the area to improve their skills, especially with respect to working with their boards. Kay designed an excellent assessment tool for the executive director and board chair to fill out, giving us the information we needed to locate organizational and operational gaps. It didn't take us long to find that most boards weren't very good at choosing the type of people necessary to make their board effective for the nonprofit. For instance, the board of a health-care program might have a handful of devoted doctors when they only needed one or two. For the board to be as effective as possible, a host of other skills like accounting, fundraising, and legal must also be represented. Kay and I learned a lot with her innovative assessment tool and, as a bonus, brought some needed help to a few struggling programs in our area. The assessments were invaluable, and I still use them today.

Graduating from Coach U, starting my coaching business, and working with Kay are just a few of the successes that gave me more confidence and the knowledge that I had experience and training that would lead to becoming an independent woman. Like you, my transformation was not a steady climb, and I even had to deal with some missing rungs from time to time, but the fire was lit. I was on a mission to change the way women see themselves, and each time I tried something impossible only to find it possible, it reminded me that I had indeed changed. I was no longer hopeless and insecure.

Branching Out

One of my favorite quotes, often attributed to Eleanor Roosevelt, reads, "The future belongs to those who believe in the beauty of their dreams."[20] As an executive director, you can build on your successes in many ways. Still, the most obvious action is to branch out and *start a nonprofit* in a niche you see missing. This kind of endeavor will take a person who can see the big picture and fundraise well. I did this as a staffer at the Women's Foundation of Colorado to form WHI. Granted, forming a nonprofit like WHI was a big jump and it may not be for everyone. But for the precious few willing to brave the journey, it's extremely rewarding to go from following orders to running your own show.

Another way to build on your current success is to *make a lateral move to a larger nonprofit* using the experience you've gained on a smaller stage. If you go this route, you'll often end up with help or additional staff you didn't have before. Your duties will primarily be managerial, focused on fundraising and working with the board rather than teaching the program directly. Once again, being a big-picture thinker is critical for this role because you'll need to be able to see down the road to keep things running so you can grow the program to serve more clients. Perhaps you'll even start an adjacent program designed to give clients additional training, like how to dress for success.

One more common way executives build on their current success is to *get specialized training as a Master of Social Work (MSW)*, for instance, and set up their own practice. In this case, you're moving to more one-on-one training with fewer managerial duties. You also get to be your own boss with all the advantages and uncertainties of working for yourself. This option is a big jump and the advanced training requires having a college degree under your belt.

Starting a nonprofit, moving to a larger nonprofit, or getting your MSW are just a few possibilities for building on your current success. But how do you decide which direction you should go in, or if, in your case, growth means staying put? I always tell my coaching clients to consider which facet of the job they're most passionate about. First and foremost, your passion should be your guide, and then and only then, begin considering the skills and mentoring necessary to accomplish the jump. Needless to say, I've had many mentors over the years. John Bell of Jonabell Farm taught me the Thoroughbred horse business. When I started WHI, I put together a group of women to meet with me regularly to guide me, brainstorm ideas, and hold my feet to the fire. Kay Irby was another mentor who taught me the finer points of nonprofit organizations. And let's not forget Letty Bass, who started me on my non-profit journey with the expertise she gained in working with the Women's Foundation of Colorado. Each of these mentors provided priceless guidance and wisdom from their years of experience, helping me refine my skills and hone my passions so I could build on my success. Can you tell I'm passionate about the importance of having a good mentor in your corner?

Mentoring can come in many forms:

1. **Peers**: Don't hesitate to ask for help from your peers, especially those who have been at the job for years and have lots of dos and don'ts up their sleeves. Most are willing to help because they once were where you are now.

2. **Funders**: Another often neglected avenue for mentoring is your funders. They likely have experience with multiple programs and know about best practices to help you leverage your current success. The best funders may even be willing to give you a grant for outside costs or, at the very least, provide you with information about other nonprofits in the area with similar programs. However they decide to come alongside you, the idea isn't to stay isolated, trying to solve all your problems alone. Remember, the obstacles you face are not unique to you or your program, and they might even have easy solutions. So, don't be shy about reaching out for the help you need. Perhaps you'll even find another mentor in the process.

3. **Fellow directors**: Fellow executive directors have already, to some degree, moved along the journey you're currently trying to navigate. And the way I see it, they are the *perfect* mentors for each other in the field and for the wonderful women they serve. Anne Lamott says it

so well in *Stitches* when she writes, "I think we are supposed to be people who help call forth human beings from deep inside hopelessness."[21] Is it just me, or does that perfectly capture an executive director's job?

The Client Path

Like you, your clients can also build on their successes. By completing their job skills training, they can immediately get a job with upward potential. Or, perhaps they can add additional training to their current skill set and then move on to a job that will open the door to safer, more independent living. In any case, your mentoring is paramount to instilling the feeling of security they lack.

As I previously noted, much of your clients' lack of self-esteem and feelings of being trapped without options are just that: feelings. Yes, it's a very real mental battle, but it's also one they can overcome by following the steps I've outlined in this book. I hope I've not implied that this is easy or a quick change; it certainly isn't. But with people like you around to cheer them on and show them a range of possibilities to build onto their success, your clients can transform their opinion of themselves into one of "I think I can, I think I can." *No matter their beginnings, with an attitude of sticking to it, guidance and encouragement along the way, they too can be Independent Women* who understand that they are and have always been enough.

A Real-Life Independent Woman
Anne Jones, co-founder of Dress for Success (Memphis, TN)

Dress For Success in Memphis started as a Career Closet out of Idlewild Presbyterian Church. Anne's deal with her co-founder was that she'd continue to be a stay-at-home mom while creating a legacy for her daughter to see what moms could accomplish together. "I wanted my daughter to see that Mama could do things to help other people." A year later, when Anne talked to Nancy Lublin, the founder of Dress for Success International, she realized that by becoming a sister nonprofit to Dress for Success, Career Closet could receive even more donations to help the community, get business cards and take advantage of Dress for Success's necessary connections. So, Anne and her co-founder spun off from the church and founded a separate 501(c)(3) in Memphis so they could do fundraising.

Anne learned an interesting fact in working with clients dealing with homelessness and the predictors of that situation. She said, "It's all about keeping the utilities on. Once you lose them, it's a steep decline. They don't realize that energy companies will usually work with you and that stopping utility cutoff is possible. Accessibility to information like this is key. We can advocate and negotiate for them with the local utility for a payment plan, for sometimes pennies, to give the client time to get things up to date. Basic needs like this are just one of the obstacles that Dress for Success addresses with their clients, in addition to the clothes they provide to interview for a job. Accessibility to information is what these clients are mostly needing. So, we coordinate with other nonprofits in the area to provide job skills training, GED certification, or even computer skills to bring our clients up to speed for being secure in their new jobs."

STEP SIX

*Recognizing Your Independent
Woman Status*

*B*ecause I was raised in the '50s and '60s, I witnessed firsthand the rise of feminism that came along with the shouts for racial equality from the likes of Martin Luther King. It certainly was a time of much pain and upheaval, but out of that came my passion for seeing women liberated from the bondage of a male-dominated society. Almost daily, I saw my mother choosing to submit to the mindset that she was somehow inferior to the men around her.

When I entered college, it was the first time I glimpsed what it was like to be treated as an independent woman. After realizing that I wasn't interested in becoming a Presbyterian director of Christian education and that the ministerial field wasn't accessible to women then, I changed my major from religious studies to political science. My thinking was that I would go on to law school after college. I found myself in an all-male department, including teachers, except for my roommate, who also was a poli-sci major. My professors, Dr. Amaker and Dr. Lacey, didn't see us girls as different from all the guys. It was the '60s, so their attitude was pretty unusual for that time. As I said earlier, when I applied to every law firm in Shreveport, hoping to get hired as a paralegal, I was completely turned down. Those lawyers were sure I was trying to take what should be a man's job, even though I was merely trying to put my toe in the water to see if I liked law. So early on, I experienced both kinds of men—those self-assured and confident enough to see women as equals and those who weren't.

Despite Dr. Amaker and Dr. Lacey, when I got married, I followed in my mom's footsteps, bringing into both of my marriages that same pattern of thinking that women should be completely submissive. Both relationships ended in my husband leaving me for another. It took many years, but therapy helped me understand that I had been psychologically abused in both marriages. I slowly began to see that there were other types of relationships that didn't involve women being treated as second-class citizens.

One day, in a session with my therapist, I found myself questioning why I liked movies like *Ava*, particularly with all the violence. In this action thriller, Jessica Chastain plays a black ops assassin who gets targeted by the very organization that employs her. I had watched the movie the night before, one of many films of female heroines conquering male villains I've watched over the years, including the DC movies. These heroines have unimaginable skills, such as the ability to take down all six men trying to kill them, as Ava did. In our discussion, I realized that my long-held motto, "Independent Women," and website (www.independentwomen.net), left over from my full-time coaching days, had been me trying to tell women and girls that they could each be an independent woman, even in their own private sphere, away from any spotlight.

My coaching media piece.

Can you imagine flying through the air looking for someone who needs your help or a villain you must take out? Or what if you were that little warrior in the first Wonder Woman movie who wanted to fight like all the grown-up women but were told you couldn't? Her elders' refusal to let her fight, of course, just made her more determined, and she even went so far as to break the rules a bit to win. She not only had guts and very little fear, but she completely believed in her abilities and strengths. That is the kind of self-assuredness we could all possess if we simply believed in ourselves and our abilities. Even if we pretend for a while, it will become more believable as we have success after success. As we learn new skills, we will discover, as I did, that some of our previously held beliefs were totally wrong, like I did when I realized I was athletic after all.

Determined not to repeat the past, in the '90s, I put my checking account in a bank called Independent Bank because it was founded and run by women. It would tear at my heart every time I heard a woman say, "Oh, my husband won't let me do that," or "I would love to, but I'm not skilled enough." Often, I couldn't help myself from responding, something to the effect of, "Oh yes, you can! I can see that you're very capable."

My Interest

I'm not interested in money or fame but rather being heard, understood, and taken as real, as a word of hope and encouragement of how to be happy, fulfilled, and even prosperous in all the ways that matter to me. Not anyone else, just me. It is doable for all women, even those who don't believe that they can get out of their current mess, to rescue themselves from the limits to the freedom of their own path. It's in our ability to soar, to see it all from high above with confidence and high self-esteem.

I hope my words, stories, and the lessons I've learned give impetus to launching your unique journey. You're an independent woman, too! You can only reach a certain level alone, but I want to walk beside you, ensuring you don't fall, that you avoid the puddles, see the road clearly, and eventually move on ahead of me to your individual road. By putting one foot in front of the other each day, you'll begin to feel a sense of being a worthwhile, loving, caring, devoted woman. It may take a long time. It sure did for me, but I hope to significantly shorten that time for you. While we may not know where your future path leads, we know it's yours and yours alone. Each new path will require us to wear different shoes and hats. Because the sun, rain, puffy clouds, gray clouds, and rainbows each require different hats. I'm transformed when I wear a hat; I feel different and act slightly changed with each one. These experiments help develop our path. I prefer a lightly traveled road because it has much less traffic and can be taken at a much slower pace. It's not as restrictive as a sidewalk feels, and you avoid the lines, even jumping over or staying out of the cracks. "Keep it between the ditches," as Mr. B, my granddaddy, used to say to imply that that smooth road was easier.

All women executive directors are *independent women!* You're strong, energetic, skilled, and caring. You've chosen a mentally demanding career that's certainly not always 9 to 5. Hopefully, you have mentors and a network of cohorts to relieve the isolation and share the burdensome responsibility. You're often working in a poor neighborhood with women whose very survival weighs on your shoulders. You must be a mother, father, sister, and even grandmother to these families because your clients are very isolated. You also function as a *coach, financial advisor, teacher, friend, and mentor.* And besides all this, you must keep "the train running" and the doors open, which is a full-time job in itself. Additionally, it's your job to keep the board up to date and enthused about their work on the nonprofit's behalf. This effort takes unique skills like balancing a budget, fundraising, and providing leadership, all requiring a great deal of self-confidence. If I haven't told you yet, I'm tremendously proud of you and appreciate the work you're doing. You're an independent woman and a shining example for us all.

The Client Path

Clients are *all* independent women, too. They have faced battles of survival, self-loathing, and sometimes even physical abuse, along with a lack of basic education and job skills to find financial stability. If there are children in the picture, the mountain is even higher because now they not only have themselves to rescue but also their little ones. Often, a church can be a temporary refuge. Mother's Day Out and similar programs give the mother the space to spend time gaining the skills she needs to survive independently. It's also worth noting that these women often take two or even three morning and evening buses to get the children dropped off and themselves to the nonprofit program. Transportation is even more difficult in rural areas because mass transit often doesn't exist. Their inner struggle with a lack of basic information, self-worth, and support leaves them in a desert of caring and nurturing. Frequently, these women are so cut off from society and the rest of their town that they are truly clueless about the help available to them right outside their neighborhood. This isolation is why churches, YWCAs, and other civic organizations must step up and put the word out about their assistance programs. Hopefully, you're networking with these larger organizations for this very purpose.

To help your clients recognize their inner independent woman, ask them questions like:

- What challenges have you faced that you're proud of overcoming?

- Have you learned anything new about yourself as you've been going through our program?

- What skills have you learned or enhanced recently?

- What's made you so determined to stay in this program and to keep on with this work?

- What's one thing you're good at and passionate about that you could use to help others?

- Thinking about the answers you've just given, are you starting to see the independent woman in you that I do?

A Real-Life Independent Woman

Emily Jo Manchester-Sanden, Executive Director of Renesting Project (Bossier City, LA)

My discussion with Emily Jo Manchester-Sanden was reassuring because it was clear to see she recognized that her path had indeed made her an independent woman. Thanks to her Master of Science in nonprofit administration from LSUS, Emily Jo started with a leg up, so to speak, compared to many executive directors. Despite her impressive education, it was often hard for her to accept her abilities and skills, so she struggled with a tendency to badmouth herself early on in her career. The lack of faith in her abilities only added to the feelings of loneliness she wrestled with. "When we believe the negative words around us, we magnify them with our own self-hate," she explained. Though Emily Jo may not have mastered all the skills she needed at the beginning of her career, she diligently worked on strengthening the areas she struggled with, like her confidence, financial literacy, fundraising, and balancing her time. These days, she sees herself as she truly is—an independent woman who's capable, resilient, and self-assured.

Today, Emily Jo and the Renesting Project are thriving, improving the quality of life for Northwest Louisiana by gathering and distributing gently used furniture and other household items to those in need. Running a nonprofit isn't easy, but the values that guide Emily Jo and her team are the "belief in the dignity of the human spirit, service before self, and partnering with other nonprofits to serve her clients well."

When it comes to where Emily Jo sees the greatest need for her clients, the most important ones are "access to transportation and knowledge of resources—like time and money—that provide that crucial safety net." If you go to the nonprofit's website (www.renestingprojectinc.org), you'll see firsthand how the Renesting Project puts those resources to work to make their clients' homes part of that much-needed safety net—a haven where children have beds to sleep in and parents can finally relax on a donated couch after a long day's work.

STEP SEVEN

Passing It On

$\mathcal{A}$s is probably evident by now, this book is the culmination of my long-held desire to pass on what I've learned through the years. My cry for the *independence of women* became a challenge to myself to do all in my power to share this understanding with others. I've lived a full and exciting life that has given me lots of time for experimentation and the chance to learn much. I'm not boring; I'm an independent woman. As crazy as that sounds even to me now, it's exactly what came out of my mouth a few months ago when I fully realized my uniqueness, strength, and power. This awareness resulted in my resolution to write this book, my last effort to claim the same for all the incredible women in my path. As you've read in the preceding pages, most of my years were spent in denial of my uniqueness and how my gifts could benefit my community. I was fortunate in many ways, but I still had to crawl out of the box of believing that I was of little worth and had no power to make the world a better place by my actions. Slowly, I became more confident in my abilities, skills, and uniqueness and realized that my years had taught me much worth sharing. I'm indeed an exciting, vivacious, monumental, and dynamic person.

I'm an *independent woman*! And the most important thing I have to say to you is that *you are too*—each in your unique way, field, occupation, or endeavor.

Although I've never walked in your shoes, I understand much of your world: how different it is and how difficult it is to get things "right." Similar to how there's nothing easy about writing a book, there's nothing easy about your job. It's hard to keep everyone happy and satisfied while doing all you can to give your participants whatever they need to move on and see their next steps. It's hard to summon the energy to do everything necessary to keep the lights on and the doors open so that women and their babies can rise. You're so busy trying to make things work and finding time for friends and family that you don't even have the time to worry about your well-being.

If you're struggling with your self-esteem or have a poor self-image, you might even find yourself with no time on your hands, thanks to allowing others to control your time completely and how you spend it. If you find yourself in the pickle of having others control your schedule, it's time to start implementing internal and external boundaries. Internal boundaries are about replacing those accusing voices of scorn or beratement with ones of encouragement and affirmation. You'll have to be intentional about stopping those thoughts in their tracks and replacing them with new ones, but with time, you can do it! Placing external boundaries means not letting your job keep you from having a full and happy social and family life. Your hours must be realistic for your emotional and physical well-being and the money you're paid. You must be clever and resourceful to prevent burnout, exhaustion, and getting to a place where you can't even think rationally because too many things are coming at you at once. Your mental and physical health are too important to lose, not to mention the mission of this organization that is so close to your heart.

Tapping Into Your Resources

While I have no doubt you could be a one-woman show, taking care of all the big and small tasks on your own, part of leadership is allowing others to step in so that you utilize their strengths. That doesn't mean you're not needed—you'll still be the overseer, director, and cheerleader, inspiring and enabling others to help and see better, bigger, and more exciting ways to enhance the program. Letting your team shine in their lanes doesn't diminish your vital role; it expands it, allowing you to lead more effectively rather than less.

We'll jump into internal self-care in a minute, but first, let's talk about one of my favorite ways to prevent burnout: asking for help—also known as tapping into the resources around you. In her book *Stitches,* Anne Lamott says, "Almost everything will work again if you unplug it for a few minutes, including you. ... If you can lean against others, none of you will blow away." Here are five tried and true ways to reach out for help by leveraging the resources already at your disposal:

1. **Track your time:** To begin addressing this issue, it might be extremely useful to track your time over two weeks, from 8 a.m. to 8 p.m. This will help you be aware of how many hours you're actually working, including weekends and evenings. Once you know your numbers,

calculate how many hours you're compensated for versus how many hours are on your own dime. Be sure to share these figures with your board so they can help you get more volunteer help or additional staff. You're only one person; if your board hopes to keep you, they can't afford to lose you to burnout.

2. **Bring in volunteers:** Volunteers are a vital part of the work your organization is doing. They want to see you succeed! Helping, no matter how small, gives them a sense of purpose and contribution—a win/win for everybody.

3. **Use your board:** The more you know about the skills and passions of your board, the better. If you're asking them to help with an area they're passionate about, it'll be nothing but a pleasure to them. For example, let's say you have a board member who loves to plan events. Then, instead of spending your weekends planning the annual fundraiser, why not let them have a hand at it? Or let's say you have a board member who's so charming that he could sell Christmas trees in January. Why not put him on the phone and have him call possible funders? If you know your board and what they're passionate about, the sky is the limit.

4. **Delegate:** You may not be able to clone yourself, but you can delegate, delegate, delegate. Are there tasks you hate performing or duties that are frankly far outside your wheelhouse? That's okay—delegate them to a board member, a funder, or a volunteer. Of course,

your direction will be needed, but think of all the time you'll save by sticking to what you do best and letting someone else shine in their lane.

5. **Start spreading the word:** Use every connection you have: board members, volunteers, funders and the media, to help spread the word that your program exists. One easy way to get the word out is to share success stories from women in your program, like the newspaper clipping I shared earlier about the single mom with four kids who went from living in her car to moving into an apartment thanks to WHI's training program. While you'll want to respect the privacy of your clients, I have a feeling you'll have some who'll be thrilled to show the world how far they've come, thanks to the transformation your program makes possible.

Small Steps To Self-Care

As an executive director, you're dedicated to the hard work of helping women succeed. You've either formed the program for this purpose or were hired to carry out this mission. In either case, your motivation must be strong because this work can be draining and frustrating, and the road for your clients is hardly ever straight or smooth. You must keep the faith to maintain their belief that the program works and help them recognize the independence and power they could have with a little training and underpinning. It's your job to bolster the clients when they show weakness and constantly reassure them that what they are attempting is possible with the right effort. Inspiring these women not only takes passion but mentorship and encouragement from your fellow staffers, volunteers, and board. When it comes to seeing these women find their passion and their independence, it's truly all hands on deck.

When I finally got firmly entrenched in the nonprofit world, I knew I had found the work that aligned with my values and fed my passion for helping women become independent Wonder Women. But even an independent woman can get tired and lose sight of what drives her, can't she? After all, inspiration can't carry the weight of failures or be the only support leg for success. We must couple that passion and inspiration with support from others, spreading the work between the staff, board, and community. With the necessary help, you can remain strong for yourself and those you serve, with reserves ready to step in when required.

Because of how demanding your job is as an executive director, burnout isn't something you can simply hope to avoid. It's something you actively want to prevent with self-care. Below are four of my top recommendations for keeping independent women fighting strong.

1. **Create new reserves:** One of the first skills I learned after experiencing that burnout firsthand was that being incredibly selfish is healthy. As Lucille Ball once wisely said, "Love yourself first, and everything else falls into line."[22] If we want to pour out of a full cup rather than one that's empty, we must give ourselves permission to be self-nurturing. But how do you nurture or love

yourself if there's just no room for anything else in your life? If you want to add something nurturing, you must eliminate something you aren't passionate about. To really care about and be generous to others, you have to create those reserves within yourself. With excess reserves at hand, people can freely take advantage of your time without any risk to you.

2. **Practice self-love:** I'll admit that self-love is hard and sometimes tricky. In her *Self-Love Workbook for Women*, bestselling author and licensed clinical social worker Megan Logan states, "A daily self-love practice sets up a pathway in the brain for self-love to become automatic, just like brushing your teeth. Scientists have learned that activated neurons connect to other firing neurons in the brain to transmit information. These neurons wire together to create a neural pathway. With daily practice, any new action in this case, self-love becomes ingrained. Sure, in the beginning, this is challenging. It feels like work or maybe even self-indulgent at times. Nevertheless, if continued, this new behavior will become second nature, allowing for self-love to grow."[23]

While it may sound like self-love is a product of having everything we want or becoming that idealized version of ourselves, that couldn't be further from the truth. Self-love comes from deep within us. It's a grace we give ourselves, a kindness we extend toward that little girl inside. It's an attitude of compassion and forgiveness toward ourselves that allows us to celebrate our wins and show grace toward the mistakes that come with being human.

3. **Speak kindly to yourself:** Many of our internal negative speeches about ourselves are just *not true*. If we are going to keep moving forward in this terrifically difficult job, we must uphold and lift ourselves almost daily with our words. It grates at me when I hear a woman speak unkindly of herself or imply that she's not good enough. Though I try to respond kindly, I want to scream— "Don't say that about yourself! You're a wonderful woman who's extremely capable and caring!" We must try to turn things around and be as caring to ourselves as we would be to a child or our beloved grandmother. Yes, we admit failures, but we also acknowledge what we learned from them with gratitude.

4. **Start somewhere:** Self-care entails lovingly protecting this woman—you—who's putting out all this effort. I realize those long hours you've been pulling may feel like just doing your job, but let me tell you from the horse's mouth, if you don't take the time to reach out even for a short lunch, or cup of coffee, the cumulative effect will be immense and burnout will follow.

So don't forget, get out and walk in a garden or park to clear your head and refocus. None of us are perfect, and we all need downtime for ourselves, even if it's just 30 minutes of self-care. It may not be perfect, but it's a start. When I catch myself attempting to make things perfect, I try to remember Leonard Cohen's song

"Anthem," which says, "There's a crack in everything. That's how the light gets in."

Taking Stock of the Progress

As you challenge old habits that suggest self-care is selfish, I encourage you to visualize sitting on an airplane as a flight attendant recites the plane's safety measures from memory. Putting your oxygen mask on first may seem selfish, but it's essential for your survival if you hope to continue serving the women in your program. I also want you to reflect on what you've accomplished in the past.

These precious women have come to you out of desperation and with great feelings of failure concerning themselves, their families, and their communities. *You have mentored* them with hope, opened the door to options they never knew existed, and you have been a living example for them to aspire to. *You have led* them to put one foot in front of the other, one tiny step at a time, so that they can not only make progress but peek into a much brighter, more independent future. *You have taught* them job skills like being on time and asking as many questions as necessary to understand the work they are being asked to do. *You have shared* your passion and underlying values while encouraging them to search their psyche and discover their values and passions. *You have coached* them to replace all those negative voices with ones of belief, compassion, patience and understanding of themselves: real self-love. *You have been that trusted friend* who's often the sightline to accepting their own abilities and accomplishments. *You have been vulnerable* about parts of your journey to prove that this transformation can take place. *You have shown them that they are independent women! You have truly passed it on.*

Will there be dropouts? Yes. Will there be backsliders who go back to that abusive husband? Yes, but they will go back having seen a glimpse of what's possible. They will never be as blind as they were before. As with addicts who sometimes have to fail many times before they have the strength to succeed, they may come again to get just a little more insight, a little more belief that they are worth it, that they can reach the top of that hill, out of their powerlessness and helplessness and into strength and self-worth that gives them the tools to find that independence they're looking for.

The Client Path

As an executive director, you get the privilege of guiding women forward into independence, self-sustainability, and a worthy sense of self-esteem. You get to help them find their inner power as they work to gain control over their lives. But if you're the poster woman for a frazzled, burned-out, tapped-out executive director, how much weight do you think your words will carry with your clients when you encourage them to take care of themselves on their road to independence? If you demonstrate these traits of self-care and a willingness to reach out for help and encourage your cohorts to do the same, then the mentoring to your participants will come from all sides, not just the top. They won't be able to miss seeing and observing those healthy practices in action and, therefore, owning those habits for themselves. Seeing the continuity all around them will offer the most substantial impact and result in a healthy and sustainable transformation.

When I think of the journey I took up Mount Massive, I believe three factors allowed me to make it to the top. As scared as I was, I made it to the summit because I took tiny steps, stopped to hydrate, and didn't shy away from asking for help when I found myself deep in the snow. A similar tale can be told to your clients to help them see that their journey is possible no matter their current fears and perceived roadblocks.

Tiny steps,
Stopping to rest,
And asking for help,
Can make it possible for us to climb any mountain in life.
By adopting these simple steps, you'll be perfectly positioned to
pass it on!

A Real-Life Independent Woman

Madison Poche, The Highland Center (Shreveport, LA)

Madison Poche is the executive director of the Highland Center, a nonprofit that works to provide solutions to those living in poverty. Since the Highland Center has numerous programs for the neighborhood, they're what I might call an all-inclusive nonprofit for the Highland neighborhood—a one-stop shop, if you will. A hub.

In my interview with Madison, I asked her if she could tell me about some common limits the Highland Center's clients face. She explained that when a client said they needed help, the solution wasn't as linear as she thought it would be. For example, if someone was hungry, she'd assumed the client could just look up where to get food and get it. Or, if someone was about to be homeless, they could simply look up the local homeless agencies and get the shelter they needed. However, Madison quickly discovered that people didn't always know where to turn for help or how to evaluate the quality of the services they could get. People were often so confused and overwhelmed that they just gave up and never asked for help at all.

"It's not just you're having a hard week and a hard time," she said. "You may not know anyone who can offer you a job. You may not have gone to a school that taught you everything you needed to know. Your family support system may not be there for you. You might be experiencing adult trauma or [dealing with] something that happened when you were a kid. So, there are a lot of overlapping challenges and ways that someone can kind of get pulled down, even if they are trying to do the right thing. As a service provider, I think having an open communication channel and building relationships of trust is how we best make our clients feel comfortable asking for the help they need. Then, we can direct them to the best of the variety of services offered." Putting this philosophy in action, Madison and the Highland Center foster that trust and open communication through meal-based programs, clothing closets, special events, and even a community library.

During our talk, I asked Madison how she trained her staff to offer hope to clients in such difficult circumstances. She responded, "I think [it's] two things. One is just the relation-ship-based nature of the work we try to do here, [which] is really important. Because isolation can be part of the chal-lenge, being a part of a community or feeling like you have someone you can call and ask for help is where hope starts. Two, I love this line from Brené Brown that says, 'Clarity is kindness.'"[24] In other words, the Highland Center (www.high-landcenter.org) strives to be clear about what they can and cannot do while simultaneously trying to fulfill client needs.

Conclusion

My understanding of the metaphor of an independent woman may be recent, but my fundamental beliefs and passions have been developing for decades under the rubric of the independence of women. The problems with equality that haunted me back in the 1950s may not be as prominent these days, but they still exist. Thankfully, women now have more work choices; perhaps, one day, those opportunities will be equal to what men get. Regardless of what is or isn't available to us as women, the things that hold us back—the forces that prevent us from seeing our real potential—are primarily internal. And, if you're like me, those internal voices are alive and well. Mix in outside factors like racial inequality, abuse, and gender bias, and it's easy to be left with a poor perception of ourselves. Put poverty into the mix and the negative impact triples. This book was designed to address this group of feelings and the deprivation of self-worth, which I firmly believe is still rampant in our society. I wrote this book for you because my arena is nonprofit organizations, specifically social justice nonprofits that serve women.

I hope what you've read and absorbed within the preceding pages has given you the foundation and sustainability to reach the unique, high-value goals you're passionate about. May you soar like an eagle as you fully own your independent woman status and help those you serve find their inner independent woman.

As Kathleen Kelly Janus said in her book *Social Startup Success: How the Best Nonprofits Launch, Scale Up, and Make a Difference*, "It's a privilege to have a leadership role in a nonprofit. It's a joy to have the opportunity to dedicate your skills, life experience, time, energy, and passion to a cause you care deeply about. That said, the work is tough and often thankless. And so, I'll end with these two words: Thank You."[25]

Susan

Nonprofit Resource List

It bears noting that there are many resources for the various facets of the nonprofit world, from fundraising to capacity building to working with boards and staff. In addition to the mentors around you, take advantage of the decades of wisdom you'll find within the materials listed below.

Some of my favorite resources for equipping and encouraging executive directors are:

- *The Coach U Personal and Corporate Coach Training Handbook* by Coach U, Inc., John Wiley and Sons, Hoboken, 2005.
- Ms. Foundation for Women (forwomen.org)
- Women's Foundation of Colorado (wfco.org)
- Charles T. and Carolyn W. Beaird Family Foundation (beairdfoundation.org)

Endnotes

1   Brené C. Brown, *I Thought It Was Just Me (but it isn't)*, Penguin Random House, 2008.

2   Chris Ordway, "Poverty Is an Empty Heart," HOPE International Blog, October 10, 2011, accessed May 24, 2025, https://blog. hopeinternational.org/2011/10/10/poverty-is-an-empty-heart/.

3   Deepa Narayan, "Poverty Is Powerlessness and Voicelessness," Finance & Development 37, no. 4 (December 2000), https://www. imf.org/external/pubs/ft/fandd/2000/12/narayan.htm (accessed May 24, 2025).

4   Eric Hanberg, *The Little Book of Nonprofit Leadership*, Independent, 2021.

5   Mim Carlson and Margaret Donohoe, *The Executive Director's Guide to Thriving as a Nonprofit Leader* (2nd ed.), Jossey-Bass, 2010.

6   Mim Carlson and Margaret Donohoe, *The Executive Director's Guide to Thriving as a Nonprofit Leader*.

7   Sylvia O'Connor, *Living the Abundant Life*, Independent, 2023.

8   Brené C. Brown, *Rising Strong*, Penguin Random House, 2015.

9   Megan Logan, *Self-Love Workbook for Women*, Callisto Publishing, 2020.

10 https://www.choosingtherapy.com/self-worth-vs-self-esteem/

11 Elizabeth Gilbert, *Eat, Pray, Love*, Riverhead Books, 2006.

12 Brené C. Brown, *The Gifts of Imperfection*, Random House, 2010.

13 Eric Hanberg, *The Little Book of Nonprofit Leadership*.

14 https://www.bls.gov/opub/ted/2024/nonprofits-accounted-for-12-8-million-jobs-9-9-percent-of-private-sector-employment-in-2022.htm

15 https://independentsector.org/resource/health-of-the-u-s-nonprofit-sector/

16 Joan Garry, *Guide to Nonprofit Leadership*, John Wiley & Sons, Inc., 2017.

17 https://en.wikipedia.org/wiki/List_of_Colorado_fourteeners

18 https://en.wikipedia.org/wiki/Mount_Massive

19 https://en.wikipedia.org/wiki/Mount_Massive

20 This quote is widely attributed to Eleanor Roosevelt, but as with the Lucille Ball quote, below, there is no specific document or speech in which she is recorded as speaking these words.

21 Anne Lamott, *Stitches,* Riverhead Books, 2013.

22 These words by Lucille Ball are frequently quoted in books, articles, online and on merchandise, but the exact origin of the quote remains vague, with no sources reliably citing any interview or memoir.

23 Megan Logan, *Self-Love Workbook for Women*, 2020.

24 Brené C. Brown, *The Gifts of Imperfection*, 2020.

25 Kathleen Kelly Janus, *Social Startup Success: How the Best Nonprofits Launch, Scale Up, and Make a Difference,* Balance Publishing, 2021.

Bibliography

Brown, Brené C. *I Thought It Was Just Me (but it isn't).* Penguin Random House, 2008.

———. *The Gifts of Imperfection.* Random House, 2010.

———. *Rising Strong.* Penguin Random House, 2015.

———. *Dare to Lead.* Random House, 2018.

Bureau of Labor Statistics, U.S. Department of Labor. "Nonprofits Accounted for 12.8 Million Jobs, 9.9 Percent of Private-Sector Employment, in 2022." August 16, 2024. https://www.bls.gov/opub/ted/2024/nonprofits-accounted-for-12-8-million-jobs-9-9-percent-of-private-sector-employment-in-2022.htm

Carlson, Mim and Donohoe, Margaret. *The Executive Director's Guide to Thriving as a Nonprofit Leader* (2nd ed.). Jossey-Bass, 2010.

Gilbert, Elizabeth. *Eat, Pray, Love.* Riverhead Books, 2007.

Garry, Joan. *Guide to Nonprofit Leadership.* John Wiley & Sons, Inc., 2017.

Hanberg, Eric. *The Little Book of Nonprofit Leadership.* Independent, 2021.

"Health of the U.S. Nonprofit Sector." Independent Sector. December 16, 2024. https://independentsector.org/resource/health-of-the-u-s-nonprofit-sector/

Janus, Kathleen Kelly. *Social Startup Success: How the Best Nonprofits Launch, Scale Up, and Make a Difference.* Balance Publishing, 2021.

Lamott, Anne. *Stitches.* Riverhead Books, 2013.

Logan, Megan. *Self-Love Workbook for Women,* Callisto Publishing, 2020.

Narayan, Deepa. "Poverty Is Powerlessness and Voicelessness." Finance & Development. Volume 37, No. 4. December 2000. https://www.imf.org/external/pubs/ft/fandd/2000/12/narayan.htm

O'Connor, Sylvia. *Living the Abundant Life.* Independent, 2023.

Ordway, Chris. "Poverty Is an Empty Heart." HOPE International Blog. October 10, 2011, accessed May 24, 2025. https://blog.hopeinternational.org/2011/10/10/poverty-is-an-empty-heart/.

Shafir, Hailey. "Self-Worth Vs. Self-Esteem: Understanding the Differences." Choosing Therapy.com. September 29, 2023. https://www.choosingtherapy.com/self-worth-vs-self-esteem/

Wikipedia. "List of Colorado Fourteeners." Wikimedia Foundation. Accessed July 19, 2025. https://en.wikipedia.org/wiki/List_of_Colorado_fourteeners

Wikipedia. "Mount Massive." Wikimedia Foundation. Accessed July 19, 2025. https://en.wikipedia.org/wiki/Mount_Massive

Acknowledgments

It's often said it takes a village to raise a child. Well, this is also true of writing a memoir. Not only my immediate family but friends old and relatively new have been there for me on this journey.

As I've previously said, I had no intention of writing a book. My sister is the writer. But about two-and-a-half years ago, in a therapy session, I discovered that the only way I was going to find closure for my life's work in transformational nonprofit consulting was to get my ideas out to more women, particularly nonprofit execs. So, a book seemed like the obvious solution.

After some research into publishers of self-help type books I stumbled upon Kelly Notaras' *The Book You Were Born to Write*. After a cover-to-cover read, I began writing. Many months and drafts later, I realized I needed an unbiased editor, so I called KN literary Arts and unlocked the door to self-publishing. I want to especially thank Becki Ruh, Sheryl Zajechowski, and Jennifer Sanders for their tireless guidance in helping me achieve what you now hold in your hand.

Because I have always been a reader of self-help books, authors like Brené Brown and Anne Lamott were essential additions to my own experience. Equally so were the advice and help from my first nonprofit mentor and good friend, Letty Bass. Eventually, I interviewed several nonprofit executive directors to add to my knowledge and—as it turned out—authenticate my words. I am grateful to all of them.

And lastly, to my readers, please converse with me via my website, independentwomen.net, and let me know what you think. I certainly don't want this conversation to stop here.

About the Author

With decades of experience and a steadfast commitment to service, Personal Coach Susan Beaird brings integrity, innovation, and inspiration to the foundation sector. Her coaching values—rooted in empowerment, growth, and purpose—help individuals and organizations stay aligned with their mission while striving for wholeness.

As founder and president of Lickskillet Plantation in Shreveport, Louisiana, Susan built one of the region's top commercial Thoroughbred breeding operations. She made history as the first—and only—woman elected director of the Louisiana Breeders Association.

A longtime insider in the foundation world, Susan understands both the public-facing and operational sides of nonprofit life. She served three years as a board member for the social services division of the National Board of the Presbyterian Church (U.S.), and chaired numerous fundraising efforts across the arts and political spheres.

As development director at Clear Spring School, an independent elementary school in Eureka Springs, Arkansas, Susan drove dramatic progress—growing enrollment from 10 to 65 students and spearheading the development of a five-acre campus from the ground up.

During her time in Colorado (1989–1998), she worked with the Women's Foundation of Colorado as an interim development associate and led the grants selection committee for the Northwest sector. Her work included on-site visits, proposal evaluations, and final recommendations to the board. She also founded and directed *Women's Home Improvement*, a nonprofit training low-income women in non-traditional skills such as carpentry, plumbing, and electrical.

Today, Susan serves as a director of the Charles T. and Carolyn W. Beaird Family Foundation, focusing on grants and community needs assessments for low-income neighborhoods and families. Her leadership in Ledbetter Heights—a high-crime, underserved area of Shreveport—included conducting a comprehensive needs assessment and helping establish a resident's association to enhance local agency and direct access to city resources.

Susan's coaching practice centers on personal and group dynamics, values-driven leadership, and fostering accountability to staff, clients, and communities. She is a certified member of the International Coaching Federation and a graduate of Coach University (CoachU).

A 1994 graduate of the Denver Community Leadership Forum, Susan continues to give back through volunteer work with The Hub and the Metropolitan Inter-Faith Association.

Her academic background includes a B.A. in political science from Rhodes College (Memphis, Tennessee), graduate studies in business administration at LSU Shreveport, and art history at Southern Methodist University (Dallas).